KB047131

처음이라도 걱정 No!

최신 기출반영 모의고사로
듀오링고 시험
완벽대비!

최신 기출 100% 반영
최근 개정 문제 업데이트!
최신 기출 내용 반영된
도서와 강의, 학습자료

최신판 실전 모의고사
최신 출제경향 전격반영
모의고사 단 3회분으로
초단기 실전 대비

DET 고득점의 지름길
120+점 목표자를 위한
고난도 문제 포함!
고득점 전략 제시까지

전문 강사의 최신 강의
유학시험 전문 강사의
족집게 강의로 확실하게
목표 점수 획득

시원스쿨 듀오링고

학습자료 200% 활용법

실시간 업데이트되는 최신 자료로 듀오링고 단번에 합격!

듀오링고 대표 커뮤니티 FREE

듀오링고 무료문제, 공부법, 동영상 강의 제공!
시험 후기 공유하고 스터디로 함께 공부해요

듀오링고 전문 유튜브 채널 FREE

듀오링고 시험의 **모든 질문 유형**을 알려드립니다.
시험 공략법과 모의 테스트 연습, Q&A까지!

사이트 온라인 학습 자료 FREE

시원스쿨랩(http://lab.siwonschool.com) 접속 ▶
교재/MP3 탭 클릭 ▶ 해당 과목 또는 교재 클릭 ▶
도서 이미지 클릭 ▶ **MP3/부가자료** 확인하세요.

시원스쿨 듀오링고

duolingo
english test
실전모의고사

시원스쿨 LAB

시원스쿨 듀오링고
Duolingo English Test (DET)
실전모의고사

초판 1쇄 발행 2022년 7월 12일
개정 2판 1쇄 발행 2024년 7월 5일

지은이 시원스쿨어학연구소
펴낸곳 (주)에스제이더블유인터내셔널
펴낸이 양홍걸 이시원

홈페이지 www.siwonschool.com
주소 서울시 영등포구 영신로 166 시원스쿨
교재 구입 문의 02)2014-8151
고객센터 02)6409-0878

ISBN 979-11-6150-612-8 13740
Number 1-110505-12120400-06

머리말

Duolingo English Test(이하 DET)는 국내에서는 듀오링고 테스트로도 불리는데, 기존의 TOEFL 과 IELTS 등의 유학 영어 시험보다 시험 길이가 짧고, 응시 방법도 간편하며, 가격도 저렴하기에 점점 국내외에서 응시생 수가 증가하는 추세입니다. 하지만 DET에 대한 정보가 너무 부족하고 온라인 시험이다 보니 수험생이 체계적으로 시험의 형태를 파악하고 학습하기가 많이 어렵습니다.

이에 프리미엄 시험영어 브랜드 시원스쿨랩의 연구진은 2024년 개정된 DET 시험을 수십 회에 걸쳐 응시하고 분석하여 최신 기출 트렌드가 반영된 3회분 모의고사 세트를 제작하여 도서로 출간하였습니다. 실제 시험을 완벽하게 반영한 본 도서는, DET 시험에 대한 완벽한 이해와 적응은 물론, 빠른 시간에 점수 향상이라는 수험생의 니즈를 달성할 수 있도록 집필되었습니다.

본 도서를 학습할 때는 실제 시험처럼 시간을 정해서 풀어보며, 반드시 Speaking과 Writing 답변을 직접 소리내어 녹음하거나 글로 써보기 바랍니다. 풀어본 문제 중 틀렸거나 이해가 잘 안 되는 부분은 복습을 통해 확실히 알고 넘어가기 바랍니다. 또한 완벽한 학습을 위해 최소 3회독을 권장하는데, 이를 위해 문제를 풀 때 정답을 책이 아닌 빈 종이에 적는 것도 좋습니다.

본 도서로 DET를 준비하는 모든 수험생이 DET라는 인생의 중요한 관문을 성공적으로 통과하여, 유학과 이민, 나아가 해외 취업의 꿈을 이룰 수 있기를 진심으로 바랍니다.

시원스쿨어학연구소

목차

실전문제 1

실전문제 2

실전문제 3

필수어휘 500

음원

lab.siwonschool.com 접속 ▶ 교재/MP3 탭 클릭 ▶ 해당 도서 검색 ▶ MP3 다운로드

| DET란?

Duolingo English Test(DET)란 언어학습 앱 시장에서 세계 최고의 다운로드 수(5억명)를 보유한 듀오링고에서 만든 온라인 영어 능력 평가 시험입니다.

DET의 가장 큰 장점은 다음의 4가지입니다.

❶ **편리** 컴퓨터로 언제 어디서든 응시
❷ **시간** 한 시간이 채 안되는 시간동안 시험을 치르고 48시간 이내 결과가 나옴
❸ **비용** 상대적으로 저렴한 미화 65불의 응시료와 무료로 원하는 모든 대학에 성적표 전송
❹ **신뢰** 전세계 5000여개 대학과 교육기관에서 입학에 필요한 영어 점수로 채택

| 시험 체계

응시자의 수준에 맞추어 난이도가 조정되는 온라인 시험 (Computer Adaptive Test)

인터넷에 연결된 컴퓨터를 통해 응시자의 정답 선택 여부에 따라 문제 순서와 난이도가 변합니다. 문제 난이도는 Level 1, 2, 3로 구분되는데, 이러한 레벨이 문제에 표시되지는 않습니다.

영역 구분 없는 하나의 시험

다른 시험들이 Listening, Reading, Speaking, Writing으로 구분된 것과 달리, 하나의 시험 시간에 듣기, 읽기, 말하기, 쓰기 문제가 혼재되어 출제됩니다.

변동성 있는 문제 수와 문제 유형

문제 수가 정해져 있지 않으며 시험 개선을 위해 새로운 문제 유형이 갑자기 포함될 수 있습니다.

| 시험 진행 순서

❶ **약 5분** 컴퓨터 카메라, 스피커, 마이크 작동 확인 및 신분증 등록, 시험 규칙 확인
❷ **약 45분** 시험 응시
❸ **약 10분** Writing Sample 및 Speaking Sample 응시

DET 시험 특징

| 채점 방식

시험 채점 방식

> ❶ **컴퓨터 채점** – 각 문제 유형에 대한 컴퓨터 알고리즘에 따라 채점
> ❷ **감독관 검토** – 여러 명의 시험 감독관이 시험 답변 녹화 화면 검토
> ❸ **부분 점수 인정** – Read and Complete, Listen and Type 등에서 정답을 일부만 맞혀도 부분 점수 인정

문제 유형별 특이점

섹션 (총 8개)	문제 유형 (총 14개)	채점 방식 및 기준
Read and Select	Read and Select	YES 또는 NO 선택 (객관식)
Fill in the Blanks	Fill in the Blanks	빈칸으로 제출하든 오답을 기입하든 특별한 감점이 없음
Mixed Language Skills	Read and Complete	빈칸으로 제출하든 오답을 기입하든 특별한 감점이 없음
	Read Aloud	적당한 속도로 분명하고 크게 발음하기
	Listen and Type	단어를 아예 안 쓰는 것보다 철자를 틀리는 쪽이 점수가 더 높음
Interactive Reading	Interactive Reading	객관식
Interactive Listening	Interactive Listening	두 가지 세부 영역으로 구분 ① Listen and Respond 유형 – 객관식 ② Summarize the Conversation 유형 – 영작
Writing	Write About the Photo	다음 항목을 기준으로 채점 ① 문법의 정확성과 다양성 ② 어휘 사용의 정확성과 다양성 ③ 질문에 맞는 답변 ④ 시간 내 충분한 분량으로 답변
	Interactive Writing	
Speaking	Listen, Then Speak	다음 항목을 기준으로 채점 ① 문법의 정확성과 다양성 ② 어휘 사용의 정확성과 다양성 ③ 질문에 맞는 답변 ④ 시간 내 충분한 분량으로 답변 ⑤ 발음과 속도
	Speak About the Photo	
	Read, Then Speak	
Writing & Speaking Sample	Writing Sample	Writing 섹션과 동일한 채점 기준
	Speaking Sample	Speaking 섹션과 동일한 채점 기준

- 자신의 레벨에 맞게 다음의 학습진도를 참조하여 매일 학습합니다.
- 자신의 레벨에 맞게 다음의 학습진도를 참조하여 학습합니다.
- 문제를 풀 때에는 시간 제한을 두고 실제 시험처럼 풀어 봅니다. 문제를 푼 뒤에는 문제를 풀면서 궁금했던 사항들을 반드시 확인하세요.
- 교재를 끝까지 한 번 보고 나면 2회독에 도전합니다. 두 번째 볼 때는 훨씬 빠르게 끝낼 수 있어요. 같은 교재를 여러 번 읽을수록 훨씬 효과가 좋으니 다독하기를 권합니다.
- 혼자서 학습하기 어렵다면, 시원스쿨랩 홈페이지(lab.siwonschool.com)에서 제니 선생님의 강의를 들으며 보다 쉽고 재미있게 공부할 수 있습니다.

| 초고속 3일 완성 학습플랜

▶ 시험이 얼마 남지 않은 상태에서 짧은 시간 최종 정리를 원하는 수험생 대상

1일	2일	3일
Actual Test (1) & 필수 어휘 Day 1-3	Actual Test (2) & 필수 어휘 Day 4-6	Actual Test (3) & 필수 어휘 Day 7-10

| 3회독 10일 완성 학습플랜

▶ 꼼꼼한 학습을 원하는 수험생 대상

1일	2일	3일	4일	5일
Actual Test (1) 1회독 & 필수 어휘 Day 1	Actual Test (2) 1회독 & 필수 어휘 Day 2	Actual Test (3) 1회독 & 필수 어휘 Day 3	Actual Test (1) 2회독 & 필수 어휘 Day 4	Actual Test (2) 2회독 & 필수 어휘 Day 5
6일	7일	8일	9일	10일
Actual Test (3) 2회독 & 필수 어휘 Day 6	Actual Test (1) 3회독 & 필수 어휘 Day 7	Actual Test (2) 3회독 & 필수 어휘 Day 8	Actual Test (3) 3회독 & 필수 어휘 Day 9	총복습 & 필수 어휘 Day 10

실전문제

1

Actual Test (1)

0:15

Read and Select

This section will have 15-18 questions. For each question, you will see a word on the screen. You will have 5 seconds to decide if the word is a real word in English.

NEXT

1

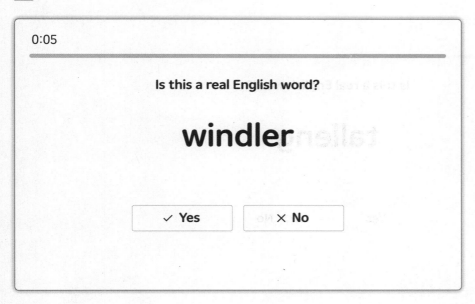

0:05

Is this a real English word?

windler

✓ Yes   ✗ No

2

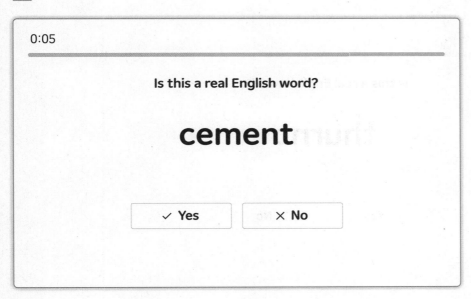

0:05

Is this a real English word?

cement

✓ Yes   ✗ No

3

0:05

Is this a real English word?

talleng

✓ Yes　　　✕ No

4

0:05

Is this a real English word?

thurnt

✓ Yes　　　✕ No

5

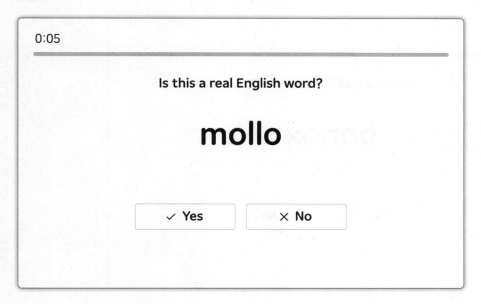

0:05

Is this a real English word?

mollo

✓ Yes   ✕ No

6

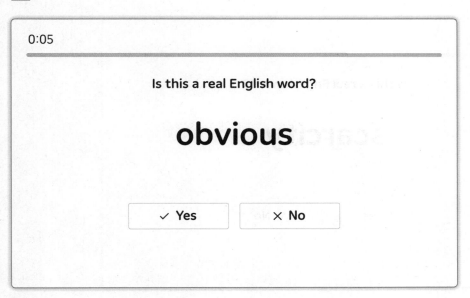

0:05

Is this a real English word?

obvious

✓ Yes   ✕ No

7

0:05

Is this a real English word?

bonox

✓ Yes	✕ No

8

0:05

Is this a real English word?

scarcity

✓ Yes	✕ No

9

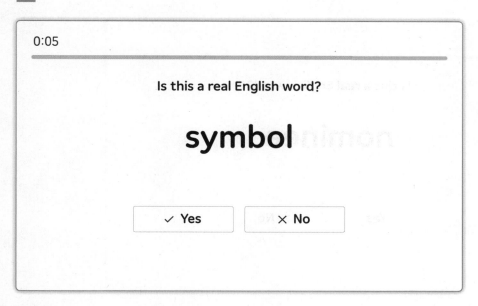

0:05

Is this a real English word?

symbol

✓ Yes   ✕ No

10

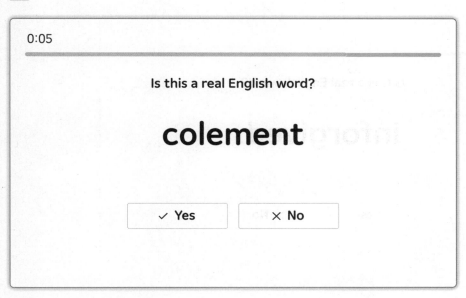

0:05

Is this a real English word?

colement

✓ Yes   ✕ No

11

12

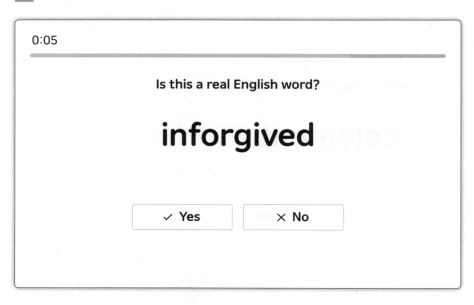

13

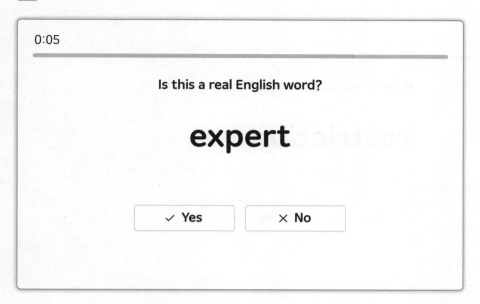

0:05

Is this a real English word?

expert

✓ Yes   ✕ No

14

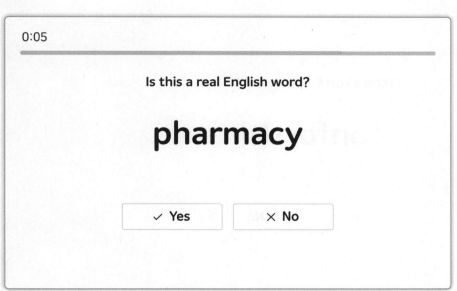

0:05

Is this a real English word?

pharmacy

✓ Yes   ✕ No

15

0:05

Is this a real English word?

restriction

| ✓ Yes | ✕ No |

16

0:05

Is this a real English word?

conforth

| ✓ Yes | ✕ No |

17

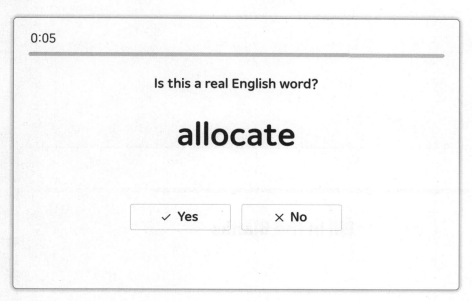

0:05

Is this a real English word?

allocate

✓ Yes   ✕ No

18

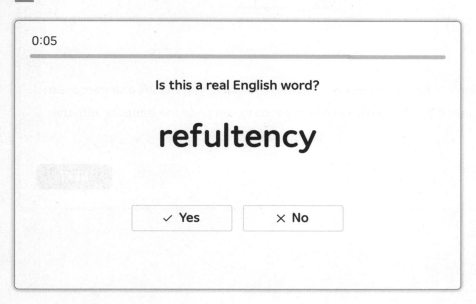

0:05

Is this a real English word?

refultency

✓ Yes   ✕ No

0:15

Fill in the Blanks

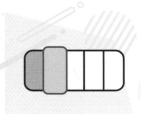

This section will have 6-9 questions. For each question, you will see a sentence with an unfinished word. You will have 20 seconds to complete the sentence with the correct word.

NEXT

1

Complete the sentence with the correct word.

The fire `u` `t` `t` `☐` `☐` `☐` destroyed the old building, leaving behind nothing but ashes and debris.

NEXT

2

Complete the sentence with the correct word.

The handmade rug had an `i` `n` `t` `r` `☐` `☐` `☐` `☐` pattern of colorful geometric shapes, showcasing the weaver's skill.

NEXT

0:20

Complete the sentence with the correct word.

One of the oldest ⬚ s ⬚ t ⬚ r ⬚ u ⬚ ⬚ ⬚ ⬚ ⬚ made of wood and stone is located in the city center.

NEXT

0:20

Complete the sentence with the correct word.

Place your plant in a well-lit room but away from direct ⬚ s ⬚ u ⬚ n ⬚ l ⬚ ⬚ ⬚ .

NEXT

5

Complete the sentence with the correct word.

The old farm was `c` `o` `n` `v` ☐ ☐ ☐ ☐ into an inn, attracting guests in search of a peaceful countryside retreat.

NEXT

6

Complete the sentence with the correct word.

Historians are `l` `o` `o` ☐ ☐ ☐ forward to discovering new artifacts from ancient civilizations.

NEXT

7

Complete the sentence with the correct word.

The real artist of the painting will always be a | m | y | s | | | | .

NEXT

8

Complete the sentence with the correct word.

The children | a | d | a | | | | quickly to their new school environment.

NEXT

0:15

Mixed Language Skills

This section will have 18-21 questions from three question types: Read and Complete, Listen and Type, and Read Aloud. It will take up to 30 minutes.

NEXT

1

AT(1)_1

1:00

Type the statement that you hear.

Your response

Number of replays left: 2

NEXT

2

0:20

Record yourself saying the statement below.

"Most organisms have a natural instinct to flee from danger."

RECORD NOW

3

1:00

🔊 AT(1)_2

Type the statement that you hear.

🔊

Your response

Number of replays left: 2

NEXT

4

0:20

Record yourself saying the statement below.

"I'll try to explain things in a little more depth."

RECORD NOW

5

3:00

Type the missing letters to complete the text below.

Jenny recently moved to a new apartment building and joined the tenants' association. Every `w` `e` `☐` , `s` ☐ meets `w` `i` ☐ other `r` `e` `s` ☐ ☐ ☐ ☐ ☐ ☐ to `d` `i` `s` ☐ ☐ ☐ ☐ `i` `s` `s` ☐ ☐ that `a` `f` `f` ☐ ☐ `a` ☐ of `t` `h` ☐ ☐ . For example, the cleanliness `o` ☐ the `b` `u` `i` ☐ ☐ ☐ ☐ , any `r` `e` `p` ☐ ☐ ☐ ☐ that `m` `i` ☐ ☐ be necessary, `a` ☐ ☐ `o` `t` ☐ ☐ ☐ issues `t` `h` ☐ ☐ relate to `t` ☐ ☐ happiness `o` ☐ the tenants. She feels the meetings have been very helpful and productive.

NEXT

6

1:00

Type the statement that you hear.

Your response

Number of replays left: 2

NEXT

◁)) AT(1)_3

7

0:20

Record yourself saying the statement below.

"They endured storms, food shortages, and outbreaks of disease during their voyage."

RECORD NOW

8

1:00

Type the statement that you hear.

Your response

Number of replays left: 2

NEXT

(◁)) AT(1)_4

9

0:20

─────────────────────────────

Record yourself saying the statement below.

"But as the scientific
community gained a better
understanding of the disease,
the earlier hypothesis seemed
increasingly unlikely."

─────────────────────────────

RECORD NOW

10

1:00

─────────────────────────────

Type the statement that you hear.

Your response

Number of replays left: 2

─────────────────────────────

NEXT

◁⑴ AT(1)_5

11

Type the missing letters to complete the text below.

Emma had wanted to visit France ever since she was a child. When s[ ][ ] fin[ ][ ][ ][ ][ ] had an opp[ ][ ][ ][ ][ ][ ][ ][ ] to go, she arr[ ][ ][ ][ ][ ][ ] a month-long trip f[ ][ ] her a[ ][ ] h[ ][ ] sister. Th[ ][ ] sta[ ][ ][ ] off i[ ] Paris and eventually vis[ ][ ][ ][ ] sev[ ][ ][ ][ ] other pla[ ][ ][ ] all over the cou[ ][ ][ ][ ][ ]. Emma fe[ ][ ] in love w[ ][ ][ ] French cul[ ][ ][ ][ ], especially the delicious cui[ ][ ][ ][ ][ ]. At the end of the trip, both Emma and her sister vowed to return to France sometime in the future.

NEXT

12

Type the statement that you hear.

AT(1)_6

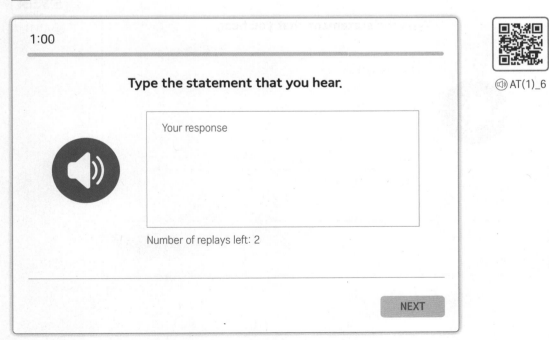

Your response

Number of replays left: 2

NEXT

13

0:20

Record yourself saying the statement below.

"If the result is still equal, extra time and potentially a penalty shootout are required."

RECORD NOW

14

1:00

Type the statement that you hear.

Your response

Number of replays left: 2

NEXT

◁》 AT(1)_7

15

Type the missing letters to complete the text below.

The 1991 eruption of Mount Pinatubo was the second-largest volcanic eruption of the 20th century. At least 16 commercial airplanes `i n a d ☐ _____` `f l __` through the ash `c l ____`, sustaining `a b ____` $100 million `i _` damage. Ten engines `h __` to `b _` `r e p l ____`, `i n c _____` all three `o _` one DC-10. Longer-term damage to aircraft `a __` engines `w __` reported, including `a c c u _____` of sulfate deposits `o _` engines. The eruption also damaged the Philippine Air Force's fleet of Vought F-8s, which were being stored nearby.

NEXT

16

Type the statement that you hear.

Your response

Number of replays left: 2

NEXT

◁)) AT(1)_8

17

0:20

Record yourself saying the statement below.

 "It has to comply with the technical standards for storing and handling hazardous materials."

RECORD NOW

18

1:00

Type the statement that you hear.

Your response

Number of replays left: 2

NEXT

 AT(1)_9

Interactive Reading

This section will have 2 reading passages. For each passage, you will have 7 or 8 minutes to answer 6 questions.

NEXT

8:00 for the next 6 questions

PASSAGE

The new principal at the ① teach / elementary / nationwide / dependent / graduate school wants to make some big changes once ② every / next / he / down / soon starts. He wants to have the ③ best / strong / most / above / good school in the area, so he has many ④ rooms / space / money / ideas / goods. He spoke ⑤ with / by / toward / gave / from the school's teachers and staff about some of the ⑥ costs / threats / students / changes / policies. The first thing that needs to ⑦ get / become / some / think / happen is improving the ⑧ city / building / park / class / education, which is getting old. The gymnasium will be completely renovated so children can play there ⑨ or / during / out / of / with the winter, and the library will be ⑩ close / below / expanded / cheap / rented.

Select the best sentence to fill in the blank in the passage.

① Select a word	∨
② Select a word	∨
③ Select a word	∨
④ Select a word	∨
⑤ Select a word	∨
⑥ Select a word	∨
⑦ Select a word	∨
⑧ Select a word	∨
⑨ Select a word	∨
⑩ Select a word	∨

NEXT

4:49   for the next 5 questions

PASSAGE

The new principal at the elementary school wants to make some big changes once he starts. He wants to have the best school in the area, so he has many ideas. He spoke with the school's teachers and staff about some of the changes. The first thing that needs to happen is improving the building, which is getting old. The gymnasium will be completely renovated so children can play there during the winter, and the library will be expanded.

_____

Children will be able to choose what to eat from a buffet of healthy options, rather than only having one choice in the lunch line. Both school staff and parents are excited about these changes.

Select the best sentence to fill in the blank in the passage.

- Another big change will be school lunches.
- It will be half the size it currently is.
- The principal had lunch with the staff.
- There was a severe shortage of teachers.

NEXT

4:09   for the next 4 questions

PASSAGE

The new principal at the elementary school wants to make some big changes once he starts. He wants to have the best school in the area, so he has many ideas. He spoke with the school's teachers and staff about some of the changes. The first thing that needs to happen is improving the building, which is getting old. The gymnasium will be completely renovated so children can play there during the winter, and the library will be expanded. Another big change will be school lunches. Children will be able to choose what to eat from a buffet of healthy options, rather than only having one choice in the lunch line. Both school staff and parents are excited about these changes.

Click and drag text to highlight the answer to the question below.

What changes to the school building are planned?

Highlight text in the passage to set an answer

NEXT

3:17   for the next 3 questions

PASSAGE

The new principal at the elementary school wants to make some big changes once he starts. He wants to have the best school in the area, so he has many ideas. He spoke with the school's teachers and staff about some of the changes. The first thing that needs to happen is improving the building, which is getting old. The gymnasium will be completely renovated so children can play there during the winter, and the library will be expanded. Another big change will be school lunches. Children will be able to choose what to eat from a buffet of healthy options, rather than only having one choice in the lunch line. Both school staff and parents are excited about these changes.

Click and drag text to highlight the answer to the question below.

How do parents feel about the planned changes to the school?

Highlight text in the passage to set an answer

NEXT

2:31   for the next 2 questions

PASSAGE

The new principal at the elementary school wants to make some big changes once he starts. He wants to have the best school in the area, so he has many ideas. He spoke with the school's teachers and staff about some of the changes. The first thing that needs to happen is improving the building, which is getting old. The gymnasium will be completely renovated so children can play there during the winter, and the library will be expanded. Another big change will be school lunches. Children will be able to choose what to eat from a buffet of healthy options, rather than only having one choice in the lunch line. Both school staff and parents are excited about these changes.

Select the idea that is expressed in the passage.

- ○ The incoming principal recognized that more children were being enrolled in the school, but there wasn't enough space for all of them.

- ○ The new principal worked with his staff to plan changes that would improve the school, including renovations and upgraded meals.

- ○ Having to deal with financial difficulties, the new school principal had to decide on several cuts that would save the school money.

- ○ The new principal wanted to prove himself as capable since the previous principal was beloved by students, staff, and parents.

NEXT

1:33   for this question

PASSAGE

The new principal at the elementary school wants to make some big changes once he starts. He wants to have the best school in the area, so he has many ideas. He spoke with the school's teachers and staff about some of the changes. The first thing that needs to happen is improving the building, which is getting old. The gymnasium will be completely renovated so children can play there during the winter, and the library will be expanded. Another big change will be school lunches. Children will be able to choose what to eat from a buffet of healthy options, rather than only having one choice in the lunch line. Both school staff and parents are excited about these changes.

Select the best title for the passage.

○ Principal Learns from Mistakes

○ Education Changes Lives

○ Budget Cuts at Local School

○ Changes Planned for School

NEXT

7:00   for the next 6 questions

PASSAGE

A health clinic, which is ① I / almost / in / just / or the same as any ② company / other / new / related / finished business, needs to hire a diverse and qualified staff. That's why it's necessary ③ and / for / the / on / you them to hire physician's assistants as well as medical doctors.

Select the best option for each missing word.

① Select a word ∨

② Select a word ∨

③ Select a word ∨

NEXT

4:49 | for the next 5 questions

PASSAGE

A health clinic, which is just the same as any other business, needs to hire a diverse and qualified staff. That's why it's necessary for them to hire physician's assistants as well as medical doctors.

_____

Physician's assistants share the responsibilities of the doctor, and as such, they examine patients, diagnose illnesses, develop treatment plans, and treat minor injuries. The main difference is that physician's assistants are not licensed to perform surgeries by themselves. Some clinics that do not perform surgeries may only hire a physician's assistant, as they do not receive as high a salary as a certified doctor.

Select the best sentence to fill in the blank in the passage.

- o A patient's medical history is confidential and cannot be shared by the clinic without permission.

- o Interested applicants must complete a 27-month long program to become a physician's assistant.

- o However, physician's assistants lack specialization in areas of medical expertise.

- o Certified doctors must spend their limited time on the most critical cases.

NEXT

for the next 4 questions

PASSAGE

A health clinic, which is just the same as any other business, needs to hire a diverse and qualified staff. That's why it's necessary for them to hire physician's assistants as well as medical doctors. Certified doctors must spend their limited time on the most critical cases. Physician's assistants share the responsibilities of the doctor, and as such, they examine patients, diagnose illnesses, develop treatment plans, and treat minor injuries. The main difference is that physician's assistants are not licensed to perform surgeries by themselves. Some clinics that do not perform surgeries may only hire a physician's assistant, as they do not receive as high a salary as a certified doctor.

Click and drag text to highlight the answer to the question below.

Why is it important for a health clinic to hire physician's assistants?

Highlight text in the passage to set an answer

NEXT

3:17   for the next 3 questions

PASSAGE

A health clinic, which is just the same as any other business, needs to hire a diverse and qualified staff. That's why it's necessary for them to hire physician's assistants as well as medical doctors. Certified doctors must spend their limited time on the most critical cases. Physician's assistants share the responsibilities of the doctor, and as such, they examine patients, diagnose illnesses, develop treatment plans, and treat minor injuries. The main difference is that physician's assistants are not licensed to perform surgeries by themselves. Some clinics that do not perform surgeries may only hire a physician's assistant, as they do not receive as high a salary as a certified doctor.

Click and drag text to highlight the answer to the question below.

What are the job duties of a physician's assistant?

Highlight text in the passage to set an answer

NEXT

PASSAGE

A health clinic, which is just the same as any other business, needs to hire a diverse and qualified staff. That's why it's necessary for them to hire physician's assistants as well as medical doctors. Certified doctors must spend their limited time on the most critical cases. Physician's assistants share the responsibilities of the doctor, and as such, they examine patients, diagnose illnesses, develop treatment plans, and treat minor injuries. The main difference is that physician's assistants are not licensed to perform surgeries by themselves. Some clinics that do not perform surgeries may only hire a physician's assistant, as they do not receive as high a salary as a certified doctor.

Select the idea that is expressed in the passage.

○ Physician's assistants handle routine duties at a clinic, allowing the doctor to focus on important matters.

○ Some clinics prefer to hire teams of physician's assistants instead of certified medical doctors.

○ Physician's assistants can attend a surgery under a doctor, but they cannot perform one by themselves.

○ Physician's assistants are more commonly hired at medical clinics since they are not as expensive as doctors.

NEXT

1:33   for this question

PASSAGE

A health clinic, which is just the same as any other business, needs to hire a diverse and qualified staff. That's why it's necessary for them to hire physician's assistants as well as medical doctors. Certified doctors must spend their limited time on the most critical cases. Physician's assistants share the responsibilities of the doctor, and as such, they examine patients, diagnose illnesses, develop treatment plans, and treat minor injuries. The main difference is that physician's assistants are not licensed to perform surgeries by themselves. Some clinics that do not perform surgeries may only hire a physician's assistant, as they do not receive as high a salary as a certified doctor.

Select the best title for the passage.

○ Diagnosing Patients at a Clinic

○ How to Become a Physician's Assistant

○ The Importance of Medical Check-ups

○ The Helpful Role of a Physician's Assistant

NEXT

0:15

Interactive Listening

This section will have 2 conversations. For each conversation, you will have 4 minutes to select 5-7 conversation turns and 75 seconds to write a summary.

NEXT

4:00   for the next 5 questions

You will participate in a conversation about the scenario below.

You are a student attending evening classes at an art college. You are considering changing the subject of your final essay, and are discussing it with your professor.

START

3:30   for the next 5 questions

Listen closely! You can only play the audio clips once.

(()) AT(1)_10_1

Question 1 of 5

Select the best response.

- ○ We usually get one last assignment in the final month of the semester.

- ○ Great! I got one of the highest grades in my entire class.

- ○ I found the multiple-choice section easy, but the rest of it was quite hard.

- ○ Yes, I chose that subject because it's one I love writing about.

- ○ Actually, I was thinking about starting over and choosing a new topic.

NEXT

3:00　　for the next 4 questions

How are things going with your final essay?

Actually, I was thinking about starting over and choosing a new topic.

AT(1)_10_2

Question 2 of 5

Select the best response.

○ The best way to prepare is to take a lot of lecture notes.

○ That's nice of you to say, but I don't think my essay was that good.

○ To be honest, I've only just started researching the life of Monet.

○ Well, it should be completed before the deadline tomorrow.

○ Yes, Monet and Renoir have quite a few similarities in their painting styles.

NEXT

2:30   for the next 3 questions

Are you sure that's a good idea? You've already done a lot of preparation for it.

To be honest, I've only just started researching the life of Monet.

AT(1)_10_3

Question 3 of 5

Select the best response.

○ I completely agree. Monet's painting style has really influenced my own.

○ That's great advice. I'll try to use some of his techniques in my next work.

○ I know, but I haven't been able to find many books about him in the library.

○ I really appreciate it. The information you gave me was extremely useful.

○ Monet produced most of his well-known works throughout the 1860s.

NEXT

2:00   for the next 2 questions

 So how come you want to change to a different topic? There should be lots of information available about Monet. He's one of the most renowned painters who has ever lived.

I know, but I haven't been able to find many books about him in the library.

◁))) AT(1)_10_4

Question 4 of 5
Select the best response.

○ I agree. I find that a lot of Internet articles have incorrect information about Monet's life.

○ In that case, I'll go to the library right after my final class on Friday and get some books.

○ I'd say he was best known as the initiator and a strong advocate of the Impressionist movement.

○ I appreciate that, and I'll try to choose a new subject as soon as possible.

○ That would be a huge help! I hadn't gotten around to looking for any information online.

NEXT

1:30 for this question

 Ah, then that might be the problem! Our library doesn't have many books on famous painters. I'd suggest checking out some websites about Monet. I'd be happy to send you some links.

That would be a huge help! I hadn't gotten around to looking for any information online.

◁)) AT(1)_10_5

Question 5 of 5
Select the best response.

○ Van Gogh? That's a good idea, but a lot of people are writing about him already.

○ Not anymore. Now that we've spoken, I'm feeling more positive about it.

○ Thanks for understanding. An extra day is all that I'll need.

○ No, I think I'll put a little more effort into learning about Paul Cezanne.

○ Thanks for explaining the correct structure I should use for my essay.

NEXT

> So, are you still hoping to change the subject of your final essay to something else other than Monet?

> Not anymore. Now that we've spoken, I'm feeling more positive about it.

The task is complete.

NEXT

1-6

1:15

Summarize the conversation you just had in 75 seconds.

Your response

NEXT

4:00 | for the next 5 questions

You will participate in a conversation about the scenario below.

You are thinking about joining a school club and discussing it with your friend. You think joining a club is a great idea but have some concerns about how it might affect your studies.

START

3:30 | for the next 5 questions

Listen closely! You can only play the audio clips once.

◁)) AT(1)_11_1

Question 1 of 5
Select the best response.

○ Well, our exams are only a couple of months away, so you'd better start studying for them now.

○ Thanks for the invitation, but I think I'll be too busy to attend this year.

○ I went on a holiday to France with my family, and we did so many fun activities there.

○ Most of the activities take place after classes, so I think you'll be able to fit them into your schedule.

○ I'm considering joining one of the clubs, but I'm worried that it will have a negative effect on my grades.

NEXT

3:00   for the next 4 questions

 Are you planning to sign up for any extra activities this semester?

I'm considering joining one of the clubs, but I'm worried that it will have a negative effect on my grades.

🔊 AT(1)_11_2

Question 2 of 5

Select the best response.

○ Good point. I'll introduce myself to him as soon as I have a chance.

○ That's what I figured. But what if it takes up too much of my time and I can't study?

○ Oh, I didn't realize you were already a member even though I know you're good at baseball.

○ I paid my membership fee yesterday, and I'm looking forward to the first club meeting.

○ Yes, it has really helped me to stay in shape, and I get along so well with all my clubmates.

NEXT

2:30   for the next 3 questions

I would go for it if I were you. Being a member of a club is a great way to stay active and meet new people.

That's what I figured. But what if it takes up too much of my time and I can't study?

🔊 AT(1)_11_3

Question 3 of 5
Select the best response.

- ○ If you could send me some more information about the club, I'd be really grateful.

- ○ It was canceled this week because too many of the members had coursework to finish.

- ○ Football? I'm a big fan as well, so perhaps I'll consider joining you for a game sometime.

- ○ You can just send an e-mail directly to the club president if you're interested.

- ○ I really like to play basketball, but I'm especially interested in signing up for the chess group.

NEXT

2:00   for the next 2 questions

 Most of the clubs only meet once a week. Which clubs are you interested in joining?

I really like to play basketball, but I'm especially interested in signing up for the chess group.

🔊 AT(1)_11_4

Question 4 of 5

Select the best response.

- That's what I mean. The deadline for the work is already getting close.

- My professor thinks I'll pass the course without any difficulty.

- What you need to keep in mind is that you'll learn a lot from attending these sessions.

- I'd love to, but I'm afraid I'll be visiting one of my friends this Friday.

- I suppose you're right. I don't typically do any studying on Friday nights anyway.

NEXT

1:30 for this question

That club just meets every Friday for two hours. I really doubt it would have any effect on your studies.

I suppose you're right. I don't typically do any studying on Friday nights anyway.

AT(1)_11_5

Question 5 of 5

Select the best response.

○ I'm sorry to hear that you didn't enjoy it. But if you fancy trying another club, just let me know.

○ Good point! I should go along this week and see if it feels like it would be a good fit for me.

○ All the other members made me feel so welcome, so I can't wait to go to the next meeting.

○ You're right. Perhaps it's not the best time to join a club when we have so much work ahead.

○ That's a great idea! I'll fill out my membership application form for the club right away.

NEXT

1:00   for this question

Exactly! And the clubs usually allow people to attend a meeting before becoming a proper member, just to see if they enjoy it or not.

Good point! I should go along this week and see if it feels like it would be a good fit for me.

The task is complete.

NEXT

2-6

1:15

Summarize the conversation you just had in 75 seconds.

Your response

NEXT

0:15

Writing

This section will have 4 writing questions: 3 Write About the Photo and 1 Interactive Writing. It will take up to 11 minutes.

NEXT

1

1:00

Write a description of the image below for 1 minute.

> Your response

NEXT

2

1:00

Write a description of the image below for 1 minute.

> Your response

NEXT

1:00

Write a description of the image below for 1 minute.

Your response

NEXT

4

5:00

❶ **Write about the topic below for 5 minutes.**   ❷ **Write a follow-up response for 3 minutes.**

There are many people from diverse backgrounds in a workplace. What are some of the advantages of working together with people from different backgrounds?

Your response

CONTINUE AFTER 3 MINUTES

3:00

✔ **Write about the topic below for 5 minutes.**   ❷ **Write a follow-up response for 3 minutes.**

There are many people from diverse backgrounds in a workplace. What are some of the advantages of working together with people from different backgrounds?

Your response

Describe a job or industry that you believe would benefit from having workers from different backgrounds.

Your response

CONTINUE AFTER 1 MINUTE

0:15

Speaking

This section will have 4 speaking questions. For each question, you will have 20 seconds to prepare and 90 seconds to respond.

NEXT

0:20

Prepare to speak about the topic below.
You will have 90 seconds to speak.

Number of replays left: 2

RECORD NOW

1:30

Speak about the topic for 90 seconds.

Number of replays left: 0

● RECORDING... YOU CAN CONTINUE AFTER 30 SECONDS

AT(1)_12

0:20

Prepare to speak about the image below.

You will have 90 seconds to speak.

RECORD NOW

1:30

Speak about the image below for 90 seconds.

● RECORDING...   ▁▁▃▇▇▃▁▁▁▁   YOU CAN CONTINUE AFTER 30 SECONDS

3

0:20

───────────────────────────

Prepare to speak about the topic below.
You will have 90 seconds to speak.

> **Talk about something you are especially competent at.**
>
> • How did you become competent at this?
> • Do you know other people who are competent at this also?
> • If I wanted to learn this skill, what would you advise me to do?

RECORD NOW

1:30

───────────────────────────

Speak about the topic below for 90 seconds.

> **Talk about something you are especially competent at.**
>
> • How did you become competent at this?
> • Do you know other people who are competent at this also?
> • If I wanted to learn this skill, what would you advise me to do?

● RECORDING...   YOU CAN CONTINUE AFTER 30 SECONDS

4

AT(1)_13

0:20

Prepare to speak about the topic below.
You will have 90 seconds to speak.

Number of replays left: 2

RECORD NOW

1:30

Speak about the topic for 90 seconds.

Number of replays left: 0

● RECORDING...   YOU CAN CONTINUE AFTER 30 SECONDS

0:15

Writing & Speaking Sample

This section will have a writing question and a speaking question. These 2 questions will contribute to your score and will also be available to the institutions that receive your results.

NEXT

1

0:30

Prepare to write about the topic below.
You will have 5 minutes to write.

> Name a famous person who you think is a good role model.
> What have they done to inspire you? What can you learn from
> this person's example?

START

5:00

Write about the topic below for 5 minutes.

Name a famous person who you think
is a good role model. What have they
done to inspire you? What can you
learn from this person's example?

Your response

YOU CAN CONTINUE AFTER 3 MINUTES

2

0:30

Prepare to speak about the topic below.
You will have 3 minutes to speak.

> What are some things that you do to show other people that
> you care about them? What are some things that other people
> do to show that they care about you?

START

3:00

Speak about the topic below for 3 minutes.

> What are some things that you do to show other
> people that you care about them? What are
> some things that other people do to show that
> they care about you?

● RECORDING...   YOU CAN SUBMIT AFTER 1 MINUTE

Actual Test (1) Answers

SECTION Read and Select

1	NO
2	YES
3	NO
4	NO
5	NO
6	YES
7	NO
8	YES
9	YES
10	NO
11	YES
12	NO
13	YES
14	YES
15	YES
16	NO
17	YES
18	NO

어휘

cement 시멘트 obvious 분명한, 명확한 scarcity 부족, 결핍 symbol 상징, 부호 nominee 후보자, 지명된 사람 expert 전문가 pharmacy 약국 restriction 제한, 규제 allocate 할당하다

`SECTION` Fill in the Blanks

1 utterly
화재는 그 오래된 건물을 완전히 파괴하여, 잿더미와 잔해만 남겼습니다.

2 intricate
그 수제 양탄자는 형형색색의 기하학적 모양의 복잡한 패턴을 갖고 있었는데, 이는 직공의 솜씨를 보여주었습니다.

3 structures
나무와 돌로 만들어진 가장 오래된 건축물 중 하나가 도심에 위치해 있습니다.

4 sunlight
조명이 밝지만 직사광선에서 벗어난 방에 식물을 두세요.

5 converted
오래된 농장이 여관으로 개조되어, 평화로운 시골 휴양지를 찾는 손님들을 끌어들이고 있습니다.

6 looking
역사학자들은 고대 문명으로부터 새로운 유물들을 발견하기를 고대하고 있습니다.

7 mystery
그 그림의 실제 작가는 항상 미스터리로 남을 것입니다.

8 adapted
아이들은 새로운 학교 환경에 빠르게 적응했습니다.

어휘

utterly 완전히 **destroy** 파괴하다 **leave behind** 뒤에 남기다 **ash** 재, 잿더미 **debris** 잔해 **handmade** 수제 **rug** 양탄자 **intricate** 복잡한 **colorful** 형형색색의 **geometric** 기하학적 **shape** 모양 **showcase** 보여주다 **weaver** 직공 **structure** 건축물 **made of** ~로 만들어진 **be located in** ~에 위치해 있다 **place** 두다 **plant** 식물 **well-lit** 조명이 밝은 **away from** ~에서 벗어나 **direct sunlight** 직사광선 **convert** 개조하다, 전환하다, 변환하다 **inn** 여관 **attract** 끌어들이다, 유혹하다 **in search of** ~을 찾는 **peaceful** 평화로운 **countryside** 시골 **retreat** 피난처, 휴양지 **historian** 역사학자 **look forward to** ~하는 것을 고대하다 **discover** 발견하다 **artifact** 유물 **ancient** 고대의 **civilization** 문명 **painting** 그림 **mystery** 미스터리, 수수께끼 **adapt** 적응하다 **quickly** 빠르게

1 Who took this photograph?
누가 이 사진을 찍었나요?

2 대부분의 생명체는 위험으로부터 도망치려는 자연적 본능을 가지고 있습니다.

3 They were all moved by his speech.
그들은 모두 그의 연설에 감동했습니다.

4 제가 조금만 더 깊이 설명해 드리겠습니다.

5 Jenny recently moved to a new apartment building and joined the tenants' association. Every week, she meets with other residents to discuss issues that affect all of them. For example, the cleanliness of the building, any repairs that might be necessary, and other issues that relate to the happiness of the tenants. She feels the meetings have been very helpful and productive.

제니는 최근 새 아파트로 이사해 세입자 협회에 가입했습니다. 그녀는 모두에게 영향을 주는 사안들을 논의하기 위해서 매주 다른 주민들과 만납니다. 예를 들어, 아파트 건물의 청결, 필요할 수 있는 모든 수리, 세입자의 행복과 관련된 기타 사안들을 논의합니다. 그녀는 모임이 매우 유익하고 생산적이라고 생각합니다.

6 The price of property is primarily driven by the law of supply and demand.
부동산 가격은 주로 수요와 공급의 법칙에 의해 조종됩니다.

7 그들은 항해하는 동안 폭풍우와 식량 부족, 질병의 창궐을 견뎌냈습니다.

8 The committee was composed of one member elected from each of the 25 largest technology firms in North America.
그 위원회는 북미에서 가장 큰 25개 기술 기업에서 각각 한 명씩 선출된 위원으로 구성되었습니다.

9 그러나 과학계가 그 질병에 대해 더 잘 이해하게 되면서, 이전의 가설은 점점 더 가능성이 희박해 보였습니다.

10 It would require a lot of focus and patience.
그것은 많은 집중력과 인내심을 요구할 것입니다.

11 Emma had wanted to visit France ever since she was a child. When she finally had an opportunity to go, she arranged a month-long trip for her and her sister. They started off in Paris and eventually visited several other places all over the country. Emma fell in love with French culture, especially the delicious cuisine. At the end of the trip, both Emma and her sister vowed to return to France sometime in the future.

엠마는 어렸을 때부터 프랑스를 방문하고 싶었습니다. 마침내 갈 기회가 생겼을 때, 그녀는 그녀와 여동생을 위한 한 달 간의 여행을 준비했습니다. 그들은 파리에서 시작했고, 결국 프랑스 전역의 다른 여러 곳들을 방문했습니다. 엠마는 프랑스 문화, 특히 맛있는 프랑스 요리와 사랑에 빠졌습니다. 여행이 끝날 무렵, 엠마와 그녀의 여동생은 언젠가 프랑스로 돌아오겠다고 맹세했습니다.

12 This control over their environment immediately promoted independence in the child.
그들의 환경에 대한 이러한 통제는 아이의 독립심을 즉각적으로 촉진했습니다.

13 만일 여전히 결과가 같다면, 연장전이나 승부차기가 필요할 수 있습니다.

14 I'll go talk to them right now.
지금 바로 가서 얘기해볼게요.

15 The 1991 eruption of Mount Pinatubo was the second-largest volcanic eruption of the 20th century. At least 16 commercial airplanes inadvertently flew through the ash cloud, sustaining about $100 million in damage. Ten engines had to be replaced, including all three of one DC-10. Longer-term damage to aircraft and engines was reported, including accumulation of sulfate deposits on engines. The eruption also damaged the Philippine Air Force's fleet of Vought F-8s, which were being stored nearby.
1991년 피나투보 산의 폭발은 20세기에 두 번째로 큰 화산 폭발이었습니다. 적어도 열 여섯 대의 민간 항공기가 무심코 화산재 구름 사이를 뚫고 지나가 약 1억 달러의 피해를 입었습니다. DC-10 여객기 한 대의 모든 엔진 3개를 포함하여 10개의 엔진이 교체되어야 했습니다. 엔진에 황산염 침전물이 축적되는 것을 포함해 항공기와 엔진에 대한 더욱 장기적인 피해가 보고되었습니다. 폭발은 또한 필리핀 공군의 Vought F-8 비행대를 손상시켰는데, 이는 근처에 보관되고 있었습니다.

16 I had already gone to bed when the telephone rang.
전화가 울렸을 때 저는 이미 잠자리에 들었습니다.

17 위험물 보관 및 취급에 대한 기술 표준을 준수해야 합니다.

18 If you had a million yen, what would you do with it?
백만 엔이 있다면 그 돈으로 무엇을 하겠습니까?

어휘

take a photograph 사진을 찍다 organism 생명체 natural 자연적 instinct 본능 flee from ~로부터 달아나다 danger 위험 be moved 감동하다, 감동받다 speech 연설 in a little more depth 조금만 더 깊이 tenant 세입자 association 협회 resident 주민 discuss 논의하다 issue 사안, 문제 affect 영향을 주다 cleanliness 청결 repair 수리 relate to ~와 관련되다 productive 생산적인 primarily 주로 drive 조종하다 law 법(칙) endure 견디다 storm 폭풍우 food shortage 식량 부족 outbreak 창궐, 발생 disease 질병 voyage 항해 committee 위원회 be composed of ~로 구성되다 elect 선출하다 scientific community 과학계 gain 얻다 hyphothesis 가설 increasingly 점점 더 unlikely 가능성이 희박한 focus 집중력 patience 인내심 opportunity 기회 arrange 준비하다

start off 시작하다 eventually 결국 fall in love with ~와 사랑에 빠지다 cuisine 요리 vow 맹세하다 control over ~에 대한 통제 immediately 즉각적으로 promote 촉진하다 independence 독립심 result 결과 still 여전히 equal 같은 extra time 연장(전) potentially 가능성으로 penalty shootout 승부차기 volcanic eruption 화산 폭발 at least 적어도 commercial airplane 민간 항공기 inadvertently 무심코, 의도치 않게 ash cloud 화산재 구름 sustain (피해를) 입다 damage 손상 replace 교체하다 long-term 장기적인 aircraft 항공기 accumulation 축적 sulfate 황산염 deposit 침전물 air force 공군 fleet 함대, 비행대 store 보관하다 go to bed 잠자리에 들다 comply with 준수하다 technical standards 기술 표준 handle 취급하다 hazardous materials 위험물

SECTION Interactive Reading

그 초등학교의 새로운 교장은 일단 시작하면 큰 변화를 만들고 싶어합니다. 그는 그 지역에서 가장 좋은 학교를 만들고 싶어 해서 많은 아이디어를 가지고 있습니다. 그는 일부 변화에 대해 학교의 선생님들과 직원들과 이야기를 나누었습니다. 가장 먼저 일어나야 할 일은 낡아가는 건물을 개선하는 것입니다. 체육관은 아이들이 겨울 동안 그곳에서 놀 수 있도록 완전히 개조될 것이고, 도서관은 확장될 것입니다. 또 다른 큰 변화는 학교 급식이 될 것입니다. 아이들은 점심 식사 줄에서 한 가지 선택권만 가지기 보다는 건강식 뷔페에서 무엇을 먹을지 선택할 수 있을 것입니다. 학교 지원들과 학부모들 모두 이러한 변화에 들떠있습니다.

1-1   ① elementary ② he ③ best ④ ideas ⑤ with ⑥ changes ⑦ happen ⑧ building ⑨ during ⑩ expanded

1-2   (1) 또 다른 큰 변화는 학교 급식이 될 것입니다.
(2) 그것은 현재 크기의 반이 될 것입니다.
(3) 교장은 직원들과 점심을 먹었습니다.
(4) 교사들의 수가 심각하게 부족했습니다.

1-3   *학교 건물에 어떤 변화가 계획되어 있습니까?*

The gymnasium will be completely renovated so children can play there during the winter, and the library will be expanded.

1-4   *학부모들은 학교에 대한 계획된 변화에 대해 어떻게 생각합니까?*

Both school staff and parents are excited about these changes.

1-5   (1) 신임 교장은 더 많은 어린이들이 학교에 입학하고 있다는 것을 인식했지만, 모든 아이들을 위한 충분한 공간이 없었습니다.
(2) 새로운 교장은 그의 직원들과 함께 개보수 및 개선된 급식을 포함하여 학교를 개선할 변화를 계획하기 위해 일했습니다.
(3) 재정적인 어려움을 처리해야 했기 때문에 새로운 학교 교장은 학교 재정을 절약할 수 있는 몇 가지 삭감안을 결정해야 했습니다.

(4) 새로운 교장은 이전의 교장이 학생들, 직원들, 그리고 부모님들로부터 사랑받았기 때문에 자신이
유능하다는 것을 증명하고 싶었습니다.

1-6　(1) 교장이 실수를 통해 배우다
(2) 교육이 인생을 바꾼다
(3) 지역 학교의 예산 삭감
(4) 학교를 위해 계획된 변화들

어휘

principal 교장 staff 직원 improve 개선하다, 개선시키다 gymnasium 체육관 renovate 개조하다, 보수하다 expand 확장하다, 확장시키다 nationwide 전국적인 dependent 의존하는 graduate school 대학원 shortage 부족 enroll in ~에 등록하다 renovation 보수, 수리, 혁신 cut n. 삭감 v. 삭감하다

다른 사업과 마찬가지로 개인 병원은 다양하고 훌륭한 직원을 고용해야 합니다. 그렇기 때문에 의사뿐만 아니라 보조 의사를 고용할 필요가 있는 것입니다. 면허를 가진 의사들은 가장 중요한 상황들에 자신들의 한정된 시간을 할애해야 합니다. 보조 의사들은 의사의 책임을 분담하여 환자를 진찰하고, 병을 진단하고, 치료 계획을 세우고, 가벼운 부상을 치료합니다. 가장 큰 차이 점은 보조 의사들이 스스로 수술을 할 수 있는 자격이 없다는 것입니다. 수술을 하지 않는 일부 병원들은 보조 의사만 고용할 수 있는데, 그들은 면허를 가진 의사만큼 높은 급여를 받지 않기 때문입니다.

2-1　① just ② other ③ for

2-2　(1) 환자의 병력은 기밀이므로 병원에서 허가 없이 공유할 수 없습니다.
(2) 관심있는 지원자들은 보조 의사가 되기 위해 27개월의 긴 프로그램을 이수해야 합니다.
(3) 그러나 보조 의사는 의료 전문 분야에 대한 전문성이 부족합니다.
(4) 면허를 가진 의사들은 가장 중요한 상황들에 자신들의 한정된 시간을 할애해야 합니다.

2-3　*왜 개인 병원에서 보조 의사를 고용하는 것이 중요합니까?*

Certified doctors must spend their limited time on the most critical cases.

2-4　*보조 의사의 직무는 무엇입니까?*

they examine patients, diagnose illnesses, develop treatment plans, and treat minor injuries.

2-5　(1) 보조 의사는 병원에서 일상적인 업무를 처리하여 의사가 중요한 문제에 집중할 수 있도록 합니다.
(2) 일부 병원들은 면허증이 있는 의사 대신 보조 의사 팀을 고용하는 것을 선호합니다.
(3) 보조 의사들은 의사 밑에서 수술에 참석할 수 있지만, 스스로 수술할 수는 없습니다.
(4) 개인병원들은 보조 의사들이 의사만큼 비싸지 않기 때문에 더 일반적으로 고용합니다.

(1) 개인병원에서 환자 진단하기
        (2) 보조 의사가 되는 방법
        (3) 건강검진의 중요성
        (4) 보조 의사의 도움이 되는 역할

어휘

health clinic 개인 병원 just as 꼭 ~처럼 qualified 자격을 갖춘, 훌륭한 physician's assistant 보조 의사, 대진 의사
certified 면허증을 가진, 공인된 critical 대단히 중요한, 위태로운 examine 관찰하다 patient 환자 diagnose 진단하다
illness 질환 treatment plan 치료 계획 minor 작은, 심각하지 않은 injury 부상 licensed 면허증/자격증을 소지한
perform surgery 수술을 (집도)하다 confidential 비밀의 specialization 전문화 expertise 전문 지식, 전문 기술
routine duty 일상 업무

| SECTION | Interactive Listening |

> **당신은 아래 주제에 대한 대화에 참여하게 됩니다.**
> 당신은 미술 대학에서 저녁 수업을 듣는 학생입니다.
> 최종 에세이 주제를 변경할 것을 고려하고 있으며 교수님과 논의 중입니다.

(음원) 최종 에세이는 어떻게 진행되고 있나요?

1-1   (1) 보통 학기 마지막 달에 마지막 과제 하나를 받습니다.
        (2) 좋아요! 전체 반에서 가장 높은 성적을 받았어요.
        (3) 객관식 부분은 쉬웠지만 나머지는 꽤 어려웠습니다.
        (4) 네, 그 주제에 대해 쓰는 것을 좋아하기 때문에 선택했습니다.
        (5) 사실, 처음부터 다시 시작해 새로운 주제를 선택하려고 생각 중이었습니다.

(음원) 그것이 좋은 생각인지 확실한가요? 이미 많은 준비를 했잖아요.

1-2   (1) 가장 좋은 준비 방법은 강의 노트 필기를 많이 작성하는 것입니다.
        (2) 그렇게 말씀해 주셔서 감사하지만 제 에세이는 그렇게 훌륭하지 않았던 것 같아요.
        (3) 솔직히, 모네의 생애를 연구하기 시작한 지 얼마 되지 않았습니다.
        (4) 내일 마감일 전에 완료되었을 겁니다.
        (5) 네, 모네와 르누아르는 그림 스타일이 상당히 유사한 점들이 많습니다.

(음원) 왜 다른 주제로 변경하고 싶은가요? 모네에 대해 이용가능한 많은 정보가 존재할 거예요. 그는 살아생전 가장
      유명한 화가 중 한 명이고요.

Actual Test (1)
Answers

1-3
(1) 전적으로 동의합니다. 모네의 그림 스타일은 제 그림 스타일에 큰 영향을 미쳤습니다.
(2) 훌륭한 조언입니다. 다음 작품에서 그의 기법들을 사용해보려고 합니다.
(3) 알고 있습니다만, 도서관에서 그에 관한 많은 책을 찾을 수 없었습니다.
(4) 정말 감사합니다. 제공해 주신 정보는 매우 유용했습니다.
(5) 모네는 1860년대에 그의 유명한 작품 대부분을 제작했습니다.

(음원) 아, 그렇다면 그게 문제일 수도 있겠네요! 우리 도서관에는 유명 화가에 관한 책이 많지 않습니다. 모네에 관한 몇 가지 웹사이트를 확인해 보세요. 링크를 보내드리겠습니다.

1-4
(1) 동의합니다. 많은 인터넷 기사에서 모네의 생애에 대한 잘못된 정보를 발견했습니다.
(2) 그렇다면, 금요일 마지막 수업 직후에 도서관에 가서 책을 빌리겠습니다.
(3) 인상주의 운동의 창시자이자 강력한 옹호자로 가장 잘 알려져 있습니다.
(4) 감사합니다, 가능한 한 빨리 새로운 주제를 선택하도록 노력하겠습니다.
(5) 큰 도움이 될 것입니다! 아직 온라인에서 정보를 찾기 시작하지 않았습니다.

(음원) 그러면, 최종 에세이의 주제를 모네가 아닌 다른 주제로 계속 바꾸고 싶으신가요?

1-5
(1) 반 고흐? 좋은 생각이지만 이미 많은 사람들이 그에 대해 글을 쓰고 있습니다.
(2) 더 이상은 아닙니다. 대화를 나누고 나니 좀 더 긍정적으로 생각하게 되었습니다.
(3) 이해해 주셔서 감사합니다. 하루만 더 있으면 됩니다.
(4) 아니오, 폴 세잔에 대해 좀 더 배우려고 노력할 것 같습니다.
(5) 에세이에 사용해야 할 올바른 구조를 설명해 주셔서 감사합니다.

1-6
I was speaking with my professor because I was thinking about changing the topic of my final essay. He thought it would be a bad idea because I had already started my preparation. He told me there is a lot of information about Monet on the Internet and offered to send some website links to me. In the end, I decided to stick with my original topic after speaking with him.

나는 최종 에세이 주제를 변경할 것을 고려하고 있어서 교수님과 논의했습니다. 교수님은 내가 이미 준비를 시작했기 때문에 좋지 않은 안이라고 생각했습니다. 인터넷에 모네에 대한 정보가 많이 있다고 말씀해주셨고 웹 사이트 링크를 보내주겠 다고 제안했습니다. 결국, 교수님과 이야기를 나눈 후 기존 주제에 충실하기로 했습니다.

모범답안 분석

도입부 내용 한 문장: I was speaking with my professor because I was thinking about changing the topic of my final essay.

대화 핵심 내용 두 문장: He thought it would be a bad idea because I had already started my preparation. He told me there is a lot of information about Monet on the Internet and offered to send some website links to me.

결론/마무리 한 문장: In the end, I decided to stick with my original topic after speaking with him.

어휘

entire 전체의 multiple choice 객관식 quite 꽤 start over 다시 시작하다 preparation 준비 deadline 마감일 similarity 유사점 available 이용 가능한 renowned 유명한 completely 전적으로 influence 영향을 주다 produce 제작하다 check out 확인하다 right after 직후 initiator 창시자 advocate 옹호자 structure 구조

당신은 아래 주제에 대한 대화에 참여하게 됩니다.

당신은 학교 동아리에 가입하는 것에 대해 친구와 논의하고 있습니다. 동아리에 가입하는 것은 좋다고 생각하지만 학업에 어떻게 영향을 미칠지 걱정입니다.

(음원) 이번 학기에 추가 활동에 등록할 계획이 있어?

2-1
(1) 음, 시험이 몇 달 밖에 남지 않았으니, 지금부터 공부를 시작하는 것이 좋을 거야.
(2) 초대해주어서 고맙지만, 올해는 참석하기엔 너무 바쁠 것 같아.
(3) 가족과 함께 프랑스로 휴가를 갔고 거기서 즐거운 활동들을 많이 했어.
(4) 대부분의 활동은 수업 후에 이루어지므로, 내 생각에 너는 그 활동들을 네 일정에 끼워 맞출 수 있을 것 같아.
(5) 동아리에 가입하는 것을 고려하고 있지만, 성적에 부정적인 영향을 미칠까 봐 걱정이 돼.

(음원) 나라면 한번 해볼 거야. 동아리에 일원이 되는 것은 활동적인 생활을 유지하고 새로운 사람들을 만날 수 있는 좋은 방법이야.

2-2
(1) 좋은 지적이야. 기회가 되는 대로 나를 그에게 소개할게.
(2) 그렇게 생각 했어. 하지만 시간을 너무 많이 차지해서 공부할 수 없다면 어떻게?
(3) 오, 야구를 잘하는 것은 알았지만 이미 일원인 줄을 몰랐네.
(4) 어제 회비를 냈고 첫 동아리 모임이 기대돼.
(5) 응, 몸매를 유지하는 데 정말 도움이 되었고 모든 동아리 동료들과도 잘 지내고 있어.

(음원) 대부분의 동아리들은 일주일에 한번만 만나. 어떤 동아리에 가입하는 것에 관심이 있어?

2-3
(1) 동아리에 대한 정보를 좀 더 보내주면 정말 고맙겠어.
(2) 이번 주에는 너무 많은 일원들이 완료해야 할 과제가 있어서 취소됐어.
(3) 축구? 나도 열렬한 팬이야, 언제 한 번 같이 너와 게임에 참여하는 것을 고려해 볼게.
(4) 관심이 있으면 동아리 회장에게 직접 이메일을 보내면 돼.
(5) 나는 농구를 정말 좋아하지만, 특히 체스 동아리에 가입하는 것에 관심이 있어.

(음원) 그 동아리는 매주 금요일에 두 시간 동안 모여. 공부에 영향을 미치진 않을 거야.

2-4
(1) 내 말이 바로 그거야. 벌써 작업 마감일이 다가오고 있어.
(2) 교수님께서는 내가 큰 어려움 없이 과정을 통과할 것이라고 생각하셔.

(3) 이 회의들에 참석하면 많은 것을 배울 수 있다는 점을 명심해야 해.

(4) 그러고 싶지만, 이번 금요일에 친구 집에 방문할 예정이야.

(5) 네 말이 맞는 것 같아. 어차피 금요일 밤에는 보통 공부를 거의 하지 않아.

(음원) 맞아! 그리고 동아리들은 보통 정식 일원이 되기 전에 모임에 참석하는 것을 허용하여 자신이 좋아하는지 아닌지 확인할 수 있어.

2-5   (1) 재미없었다고 들으니 유감이네. 하지만 다른 동아리에 도전하고 싶다면 알려줘.

(2) 좋은 지적이야! 이번 주에 가서 나에게 잘 맞는지 확인해 봐야겠어.

(3) 모든 일원들이 너무 환영해줘서 다음 모임까지 기다리는 게 기대돼.

(4) 네가 맞아. 앞으로 해야 할 일이 너무 많은 지금이 동아리에 가입하기에 가장 좋은 시기는 아닐 수도 있어.

(5) 정말 좋은 생각이야! 바로 동아리 가입 신청서를 작성할게.

2-6   I was speaking with my friend about joining a club at our school. She thought it was a great idea and told me it would be a good way to stay active and make friends. However, I was worried it would have a bad effect on my schoolwork. In the end, I decided to go to a club meeting to decide if I would like to join or not.

나는 우리 학교 동아리에 가입하는 것에 대해 친구와 이야기를 하고 있었습니다. 친구는 좋은 생각이라고 생각했고 활동적인 생활을 유지하고 새로운 사람들을 만날 수 있는 좋은 방법이라고 말해줬습니다. 하지만, 나는 학업에 나쁜 영향을 미칠까봐 걱정했습니다. 결국, 나는 동아리 모임에 참석하여 가입 여부를 결정하기로 했습니다.

모범답안 분석

도입부 내용 한 문장: I was speaking with my friend about joining a club at our school.

대화 핵심 내용 두 문장: She thought it was a great idea and told me it would be a good way to stay active and make friends. However, I was worried it would have a bad effect on my schoolwork.

결론/마무리 한 문장: In the end, I decided to go to a club meeting to decide if I would like to join or not.

어휘

sign up for ~에 등록하다 **invitation** 초대 **attend** 참석하다 **introduce** 소개하다 **take up** 차지하다 **grateful** 고마워하는 **cancel** 취소하다 **coursework** 과제 **president** 회장 **course** (수업) 과정 **keep in mind** 명심하다 **allow** 허용하다 **application** 신청서 **schoolwork** 학업

1   This is a photograph of two bicycles in the woods. In detail, one of the bicycles is pink, and the other one is green. On top of that, it looks like it is a bright, sunny day.

이것은 숲속에 있는 두 자전거에 대한 사진입니다. 자세히 보면, 자전거 한 대는 핑크색이고 다른 것은 녹색입니다. 또한, 밝은 화창한 날처럼 보입니다.

2   This is a photograph of a person giving a speech in front of a lot of people. In detail, he is on a stage on top of a red vehicle. In front of him, there is a crowd listening to his speech. In the background, there is a tall brick building with many windows.

이것은 많은 사람들 앞에서 연설하는 사람의 사진입니다. 자세히 보면, 그는 빨간색 차량 위에 있는 무대에 서 있습니다. 그 앞에는 그의 연설을 듣고 있는 군중이 있습니다. 배경에는, 많은 창문의 높은 벽돌 건물이 있습니다.

3   This is a photograph of three ladies wearing a dress. In detail, the lady on the left is wearing a green dress, and she is looking down. The lady in the middle is in a light blue dress, and she has dark, medium-length hair. Next to her, there is a lady with blonde hair and a beige hat.

이것은 드레스를 입은 세 여성의 사진입니다. 자세히 보면 왼쪽에 있는 여성은 녹색 드레스를 입고 아래를 내려다보고 있습니다. 가운데에 있는 여성은 하늘색 드레스를 입고 있으며 짙은 중간 길이의 머리를 하고 있습니다. 그 옆에는, 금발 머리에 베이지색 모자를 쓴 여성이 있습니다.

4   ① 직장에는 다양한 배경을 가진 사람들이 많이 있습니다. 다양한 배경을 가진 사람들과 함께 일할 때 어떤 이점이 있습니까?

These days, it is easy to find workplaces that have people from various backgrounds. The two most prominent advantages are improving social skills and broadening horizons. First, working with people from different backgrounds allows you to improve the ability to interact and cooperate with various people. This is because you have to know how to communicate with a diverse group of people. Second, it is easy to extend your horizons by working with various types of people. You can get a chance to hear different opinions of people from different backgrounds. This allows you to think in a new perspective. To conclude, working with people from different backgrounds is advantageous.

요즘은, 다양한 배경을 가진 사람들이 함께 일하는 직장을 쉽게 찾을 수 있습니다. 가장 눈에 띄는 두 가지 장점은 사회성 능력을 향상시키는 것과 시야를 확대하는 것입니다. 첫째, 다양한 배경을 가진 사람들과 함께 일하면 다양한 사람들과 교류하고 협력하는 능력을 향상시킬 수 있습니다. 다양한 사람들과 소통하는 방법을 알아야 하기 때문입니다. 둘째, 다양한 유형의 사람들과 함께 일함으로써 시야를 넓힐 수 있습니다. 다양한 배경을 가진 사람들의 다양한 의견을 들을 수 있는 기회를 얻을 수 있습니다. 이를 통해 새로운 시각으로 생각할 수 있습니다. 결론적으로, 다양한 배경을 가진 사람들과 함께 일하는 것이 유리합니다.

② 다양한 배경을 가진 근로자를 채용하면 도움이 될 것으로 생각되는 직업 또는 산업에 대해 설명하세요.

One industry that would significantly benefit from having workers from different backgrounds is marketing. A diverse marketing team can give valuable insight into cultural preferences and sensitivities. Thus, they can create advertisements that successfully target a large audience.

다양한 배경을 가진 직원이 있으면 큰 이점을 얻을 수 있는 산업 중 하나는 마케팅입니다. 다양한 배경을 가진 마케팅 팀은 문화적 선호도와 감수성에 대한 귀중한 통찰력을 제공할 수 있습니다. 따라서 많은 대상(잠재 고객)을 성공적으로 타겟팅하는 광고를 만들 수 있습니다.

어휘

woods 숲 give a speech 연설하다 stage 무대 vehicle 차량 crowd 군중 brick 벽돌 look down 내려다보다 light blue 하늘색 dark 짙은 medium-length 중간 길이의 blonde 금발 beige 베이지색 prominent 눈에 띄는, 현저한 improve 향상시키다 social skills 사회성 기술 broaden 넓히다 extend 넓히다 horizon 시야 interact 교류하다 cooperate 협력하다 perspective 시각 advantageous 유리한 significantly 크게, 상당하게 benefit from ~로부터 이점을 얻다 insight 통찰력 preference 선호도 sensitivity 감수성 create 만들다 audience 대상, 관중, 청중

 SECTION Speaking

1 *What are the advantages and disadvantages of having a large family?
대가족을 갖는 것의 장점과 단점은 무엇입니까?*

There are several advantages and disadvantages of having a large family. One of the advantages is that you can learn how to get along with different types of people since each member in a large family has a different personality. This experience can be useful when you join a larger community. On the other hand, having a large family can have some disadvantages. One that comes to mind is that it can be stressful to have too many people at home all the time. In detail, if there are too many people at home, family members will have a lack of privacy. Therefore, I think having a large family has both benefits and drawbacks.

대가족을 갖는 것에는 몇 가지 장점과 단점이 있습니다. 장점들 중 하나는 사람들이 자연스럽게 다양한 유형의 사람들과 잘지내는 법을 배울 수 있다는 점인데, 대가족에는 각 구성원이 다른 성격을 갖고 있기 때문입니다. 이러한 경험은 더 큰 공동체에 합류할 때 유용할 수 있습니다. 반면에, 대가족은 몇 가지 단점이 있을 수 있습니다. 가장 먼저 떠오르는 것은 집에 항상 너무 많은 사람이 있으면 스트레스를 받을 수 있다는 것입니다. 구체적으로, 집에 사람이 너무 많으면 가족 구성원의 프라이버시가 부족해집니다. 따라서, 대가족을 갖는 것은 장점과 단점 둘 다 있다고 생각합니다.

2 This is a picture of two men standing and looking in opposite directions. In detail, I can see that the man in the foreground is wearing a white sleeveless T-shirt. On top of that, he is smiling. From this, I can infer that he is happy about something. And in the background, the other man is facing a pond. This clearly shows that he is pumping water out of the pond.

이것은 두 남자가 서서 서로 반대 방향을 바라보는 사진입니다. 자세히 보면 전경에 있는 남성이 흰색 민소매 티셔츠를 입고 있는 것을 볼 수 있습니다. 게다가, 그는 웃고 있습니다. 이를 통해 그가 무언가에 대해 행복하다는 것을 유추할 수 있습니다. 그리고 배경에서 다른 남자는 못을 바라보고 있습니다. 이것은 그가 못에서 물을 퍼내고 있다는 것을 분명히 보여줍니다.

3 *당신이 특히 잘하는 것에 대해 이야기하십시오.*
  · *어떻게 이것을 잘하게 되었습니까?*
  · *이것을 잘 하는 다른 사람들도 알고 있습니까?*
  · *제가 이 능력을 배우고 싶다면, 무엇을 하라고 조언해 주시겠습니까?*

I am especially competent at communicating with others in any given situation. To give you more detail, I always listen to others first before stating my argument or opinion. By doing so, I can get a chance to understand others thoroughly and elaborate on my opinion from what they say. This reduces misunderstandings when communicating with others. I know that my mother is competent at this, and I think I learned this skill from her. If you wanted to learn this skill, I would advise you to remember to listen to others' opinions first. On top of that, I would also tell you to show positive reactions towards others when communicating.

저는 어떠한 주어진 상황에서도 다른 사람들과 의사소통을 특히 잘 합니다. 좀 더 자세히 말씀드리자면, 저는 제 주장이나 의견을 말하기 전에 항상 먼저 다른 사람의 말을 경청합니다. 그렇게 함으로써, 저는 다른 사람들을 충분히 이해하고 그들이 말한 것으로부터 제 의견을 정교하게 만들 수 있습니다. 이것은 다른 사람들과 소통할 때 오해의 가능성을 줄입니다. 저는제 어머니가 이것을 잘한다는 것을 알고 있고 제가 어머니에게서 이 능력을 배웠다고 생각합니다. 이 능력을 배우고 싶다면, 먼저 다른 사람의 의견을 듣는 것을 잊지 말라고 조언하겠습니다. 또한, 소통할 때에도 상대방에게 긍정적인 반응을 보이라고 말씀드리겠습니다.

4 *How should governments encourage people to eat more healthily?*
사람들이 더 건강하게 먹도록 정부가 어떻게 장려해야 합니까?

There are many different ways that governments can encourage people to eat healthier. However, in my opinion, the best way is to make informational videos on healthy eating. In detail, the videos should show the negative effects of eating unhealthy food. From this, people can become aware of the consequences of not eating clean food, and it is likely that they will try to change their diet. In addition, people nowadays are exposed to a lot of media. Therefore, promoting a healthy diet using the media is an effective way to make people pursue a clean diet.

정부가 사람들이 더 건강한 식습관을 갖도록 장려할 수 있는 방법은 여러 가지가 있습니다. 하지만, 제 생각에 가장 좋은 방법은 건강한 식습관에 대한 정보를 담은 영상을 만드는 것입니다. 구체적으로, 영상은 건강에 해로운 음식 섭취의 부정적인 영향을 자세히 보여줘야 합니다. 이를 통해, 사람들은 깨끗한 음식을 먹지 않을 때의 결과를 인식 할 수 있으며 식단을 바꾸려고 노력할 가능성이 높습니다. 또한 요즘 사람들은 많은 미디어에 노출되어 있습니다. 따라서 미디어를 통해 건강한 식단을 홍보하는 것은 사람들이 깨끗한 식단을 추구하도록 만드는 효과적인 방법입니다.

어휘

large family 대가족(다자녀 가정) get along with ~와 잘 지내다 family member 가족 구성원 personality 성격 community 공동체 come to mind 생각이 떠오르다 lack 부족 privacy 프라이버시, 사생활 benefit 장점, 이익 drawback 단점, 문제점 in opposite directions 반대 방향으로 foreground 전경 sleeveless 민소매 infer 유추하다 face 바라보다, 향하다 pond 못, 연못 pump out (펌프질로) 퍼내다 competent 능숙한, 잘하는 skill 능력, 기술 advise 조언하다 especially 특히 communicate 의사소통을 하다 state 말하다 argument 주장 opinion 의견 thoroughly 완전히 elaborate 더 자세히 설명하다 reduce 줄이다 misunderstand 오해하다 positive reaction 긍정적인 반응 encourage 장려하다 informational 정보를 담은 healthy eating 건강한 식습관 be aware of 인식하다 consequence 결과 diet 식단 be exposed to ~에 노출되다 pursue 추구하다 clean diet 깨끗한 식단

SECTION   Writing & Speaking Sample

1   *당신이 좋은 롤모델이라고 생각하는 유명인의 이름을 말하십시오. 그들이 당신에게 어떤 영감을 주었나요? 그 사람의 예에서 무엇을 배울 수 있습니까?*

Personally, the famous person I admire the most is Steve Jobs, the founder of Apple. The reason why I think he is an inspiring figure is that he has had several accomplishments. One of them is that he created and developed the iPhone, a widely used smartphone. This could have been only possible through devoting all his time and efforts into his work. Furthermore, he was an influential figure in many aspects. In my perspective, having passion in one's job is the driving factor, and Jobs was a passionate man. I also strive to be successful in my career. Therefore, I hope to follow in the footsteps of Jobs.

개인적으로 제가 가장 존경하는 사람은 애플의 창업자인 스티브 잡스입니다. 제가 그를 영감을 주는 인물이라고 생각하는 이유는 그가 여러 가지 업적을 남겼기 때문입니다. 그 중 하나는 그가 널리 사용되는 스마트폰인 아이폰을 만들고 개발했다는 것입니다. 이것은 그가 모든 시간과 노력을 자신의 일에 바쳤을 때만 가능했습니다. 게다가, 그는 많은 면에서 영향력 있는 인물이었습니다. 제 관점에서, 일에 열정을 가지는 것은 원동력이고 잡스는 열정적인 사람이었습니다. 저 또한 제 직업에서 성공하기 위해 정진합니다. 그러므로 저는 잡스의 전철을 밟고 싶습니다.

2   *다른 사람들에게 당신이 그들을 아끼고 있다는 것을 보여주기 위해 하는 일은 무엇입니까? 다른 사람들이*

당신을 아끼고 있다는 것을 보여주기 위해 하는 행동에는 어떤 것들이 있습니까?

There are many different ways to show others that you care about them. However, in my case, I tend to buy gifts for my friends. Whenever they feel depressed, I try my best to look for things that might make them delighted. For instance, when one of my friends was sick, I bought chicken soup for them. This made them feel that they were being cared for. On the other hand, what others have done to show me that they care about me is that they have written letters on special days such as my birthday. Also, some other people have texted me or called me when I was having a hard time. To conclude, I think there are many different ways to show that you care about others.

다른 사람들에게 여러분이 그들을 아끼고 있다는 것을 보여주는 많은 다른 방법들이 있습니다. 하지만 저 같은 경우에는 친구들에게 줄 선물을 사는 편입니다. 그들이 우울해할 때마다, 저는 그들을 즐겁게 해줄 수 있는 것들을 찾기 위해 최선을 다합니다. 예를 들어, 내 친구 중 한 명이 아플 때, 나는 그녀를 위해 닭고기 수프를 샀습니다. 이것은 그녀가 보살핌을 받고 있다고 느끼게 했습니다. 반면에, 다른 사람들이 저를 아낀다는 것을 보여주기 위해 한 일은 그들이 제 생일과 같은 특별한 날에 편지를 썼다는 것입니다. 또한, 다른 몇몇 사람들은 제가 어려운 시기를 보낼 때 저에게 문자나 전화를 했습니다. 결론적으로, 저는 여러분이 다른 사람들을 아낀다는 것을 보여주는 많은 다른 방법들이 있다고 생각합니다.

어휘

role model 롤모델, 모범이 되는 사람 inspire 고무하다, 영감을 주다 example 본보기 admire 존경하다 founder 창업자 accomplishment 업적 devote (몸, 돈, 노력, 시간 등을) 바치다, 쏟다 time and effort 시간과 노력 furthermore 뿐만 아니라, 더욱이 influential 영향력 있는 figure 숫자, 인물 perspective 관점 driving factor 원동력 passionate 열정적인 strive 정진하다, 매진하다 follow in the footsteps of ~의 뒤를 따르다 care about[for] ~에 마음을 쓰다 tend to ~하는 경향이 있다 depressed 우울한 delighted 아주 기뻐하는, 아주 즐거워하는 text 문자를 보내다 hard time 어려운 시기

실전문제

2

Actual Test (2)

Read and Select

This section will have 15-18 questions. For each question, you will see a word on the screen. You will have 5 seconds to decide if the word is a real word in English.

NEXT

1

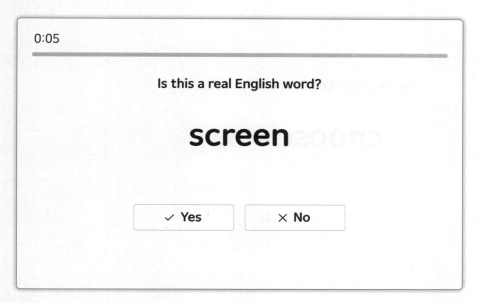

0:05

Is this a real English word?

screen

✓ Yes   ✕ No

2

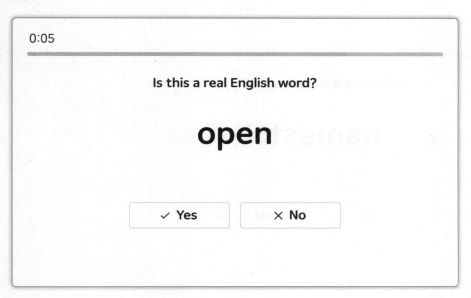

0:05

Is this a real English word?

open

✓ Yes   ✕ No

3

0:05

Is this a real English word?

choose

✓ Yes   ✕ No

4

0:05

Is this a real English word?

nemest

✓ Yes   ✕ No

5

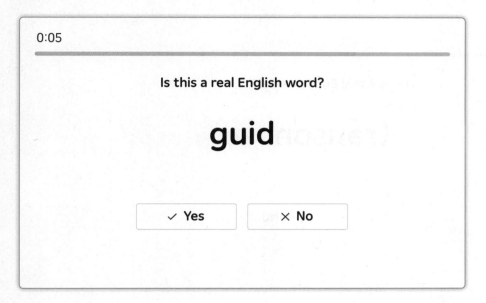

0:05

Is this a real English word?

guid

✓ Yes   ✕ No

6

0:05

Is this a real English word?

giving

✓ Yes   ✕ No

7

> 0:05
>
> ---
>
> **Is this a real English word?**
>
> # trauson
>
> ✓ Yes   ✕ No

8

> 0:05
>
> ---
>
> **Is this a real English word?**
>
> # overn
>
> ✓ Yes   ✕ No

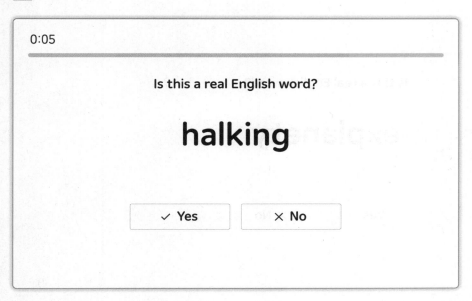

0:05

Is this a real English word?

halking

✓ Yes   ✕ No

0:05

Is this a real English word?

heeper

✓ Yes   ✕ No

11

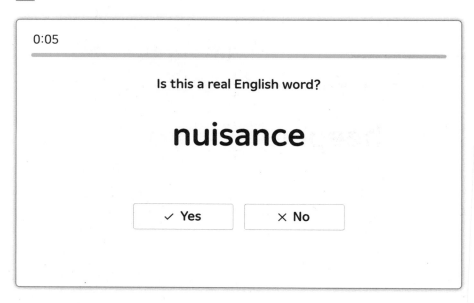

0:05

Is this a real English word?

explanety

✓ Yes   ✕ No

12

0:05

Is this a real English word?

nuisance

✓ Yes   ✕ No

13

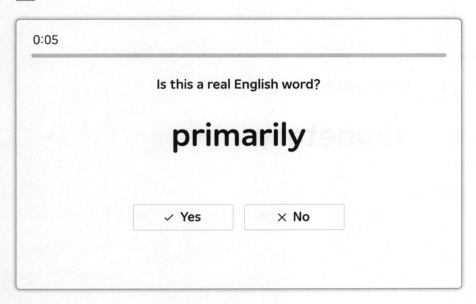

0:05

Is this a real English word?

primarily

✓ Yes   ✕ No

14

0:05

Is this a real English word?

frait

✓ Yes   ✕ No

15

0:05

Is this a real English word?

monetary

| ✓ Yes | ✕ No |

16

0:05

Is this a real English word?

fraudulent

| ✓ Yes | ✕ No |

17

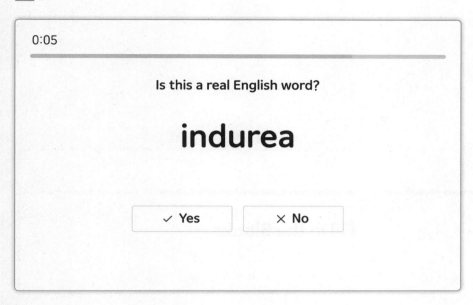

0:05

Is this a real English word?

indurea

✓ Yes   ✕ No

18

0:05

Is this a real English word?

uncointic

✓ Yes   ✕ No

Fill in the Blanks

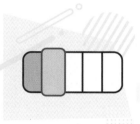

This section will have 6-9 questions. For each question, you will see a sentence with an unfinished word. You will have 20 seconds to complete the sentence with the correct word.

NEXT

1

0:20

Complete the sentence with the correct word.

His c h ☐ ☐ made him a favorite among the group's fans.

NEXT

2

0:20

Complete the sentence with the correct word.

Their footsteps in the snow m a r ☐ ☐ the path they had taken through the forest.

NEXT

3

Complete the sentence with the correct word.

She looked at him | s | q | u | | | | | in the eye and asked to hear
everything, even the smallest details.

NEXT

4

Complete the sentence with the correct word.

| P | e | r | | | | it's time for me to step out of my comfort zone and pursue
my passion for acting.

NEXT

5

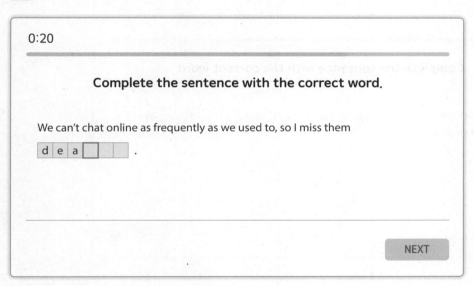

0:20

Complete the sentence with the correct word.

Evaluating the feasibility of implementing a policy is crucial to avoid the need

to c a n ⬚ ⬚ it.

NEXT

6

0:20

Complete the sentence with the correct word.

We can't chat online as frequently as we used to, so I miss them

d e a ⬚ ⬚ .

NEXT

7

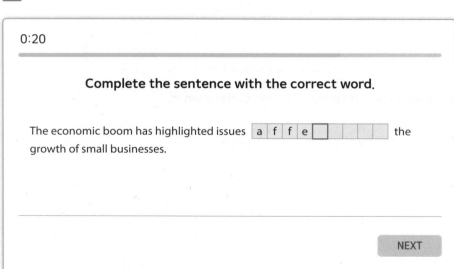

0:20

Complete the sentence with the correct word.

Before starting your final project, schedule a
| c | o | n | s | u | | | | | | | with your professor to brainstorm ideas
and get feedback.

NEXT

8

0:20

Complete the sentence with the correct word.

The economic boom has highlighted issues | a | f | f | e | | | | the
growth of small businesses.

NEXT

0:15

Mixed Language Skills

This section will have 18-21 questions from three question types: Read and Complete, Listen and Type, and Read Aloud. It will take up to 30 minutes.

NEXT

1:00

Type the statement that you hear.

Your response

Number of replays left: 2

NEXT

📢 AT(2)_1

0:20

Record yourself saying the statement below.

"I'd like to keep attending the classes."

RECORD NOW

3

1:00

Type the statement that you hear.

🔊 AT(2)_2

Your response

Number of replays left: 2

NEXT

4

0:20

Record yourself saying the statement below.

"The earliest settlers took advantage of the abundance of seafood they had access to in the coastal waters."

RECORD NOW

5

3:00

Type the missing letters to complete the text below.

The Millennium Bridge i [ ] a footbridge across the River Thames in London.
It is a s t [ ][ ][ ] suspension b r i [ ][ ][ ] which l i [ ]
Bankside w i [ ][ ] the city. Its p o s i [ ][ ][ ] is
b e t [ ][ ][ ][ ] Southwark Bridge (d o w n [ ][ ][ ][ ][ ])
a [ ] Blackfriars Railway Bridge (upstream). The b r i [ ][ ][ ]
opened o [ ] 10 June 2000. It is the newest bridge across the Thames.

NEXT

6

1:00

Type the statement that you hear.

Your response

Number of replays left: 2

NEXT

AT(2)_3

7

0:20

Record yourself saying the statement below.

"The book was published with several different front covers, each of which depicted a different character."

RECORD NOW

8

1:00

Type the statement that you hear.

Your response

Number of replays left: 2

NEXT

AT(2)_4

9

0:20

Record yourself saying the statement below.

"Next week, the electrician will come and fix the cable."

RECORD NOW

10

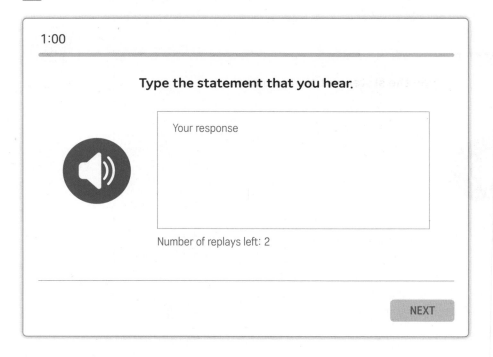

1:00

Type the statement that you hear.

Your response

Number of replays left: 2

NEXT

AT(2)_5

11

Type the missing letters to complete the text below.

Comet Leonard was discovered by astronomer Gregory J. Leonard on January 3 at the Mount Lemmon Observatory. The observatory `i` located `o` Mount Lemmon in `t` Santa Catalina Mountains, `a p p r` 25 kilometers northeast `o` Tucson, Arizona. When Mr. Leonard `f o` the comet's image, it `w` a faint `o b j` of magnitude 19. That `i` nearly 160,000 times `d i m` than the faintest stars `v i s` to the unaided `e`. However, there is a chance that the comet will be seen clearly at its nearest point to Earth.

NEXT

12

1:00

Type the statement that you hear.

Your response

Number of replays left: 2

NEXT

AT(2)_6

13

0:20

Record yourself saying the statement below.

"People usually sign a contract when something important or costly is being done."

RECORD NOW

14

1:00

Type the statement that you hear.

Your response

Number of replays left: 2

NEXT

AT(2)_7

15

3:00

Type the missing letters to complete the text below.

Gregory: What is included in the meal special?

Waiter: If [y] order a large [p][a] , you'll get a salad [a] drink [f] free.

Gregory: I'll [t][a] the [p][a] , [b] can [y] tell [t] cook [t] add [o][l][i] , please?

Waiter: Unfortunately, you can't add anything to the pasta and still get the free stuff.

NEXT

16

1:00

Type the statement that you hear.

Your response

Number of replays left: 2

NEXT

◀) AT(2)_8

17

0:20

Record yourself saying the statement below.

 "The process of making beer is known as brewing."

RECORD NOW

18

1:00

Type the statement that you hear.

Your response

Number of replays left: 2

NEXT

 AT(2)_9

0:15

Interactive Reading

This section will have 2 reading passages. For each passage, you will have 7 or 8 minutes to answer 6 questions.

NEXT

7:00   for the next 6 questions

PASSAGE

When I was growing up, I often ① broke / got / threw / walked / took into a ② plenty / some / lot / number / many of trouble because of one of my ③ methods / classes / mistakes / habits / deals. I would open all the windows in my room when it was hot in the summer. It was dangerous because we lived on the first floor, so my mom would ④ that / she / do / too / be worried about my safety. Still, ⑤ it / these / mom / hers did cool down our home and saved us money on electricity. Now, as an adult, I'm finally going to buy an air conditioner.

Select the best sentence to fill in the blank in the passage.

① Select a word	∨
② Select a word	∨
③ Select a word	∨
④ Select a word	∨
⑤ Select a word	∨

NEXT

3:49   for the next 5 questions

PASSAGE

When I was growing up, I often got into a lot of trouble because of one of my habits. I would open all the windows in my room when it was hot in the summer. It was dangerous because we lived on the first floor, so my mom would be worried about my safety. Still, it did help cool down our home and saved us money on electricity. Now, as an adult, I'm finally going to buy an air conditioner.

However, since I have children of my own now, I need to make sure that they're comfortable and safe.

Select the best sentence to fill in the blank in the passage.

- ○ It's like my house is always cold, no matter what season it is.

- ○ I know it will be expensive, especially in the hot summer months.

- ○ My brother recommended this unit because it works so well in his home.

- ○ Constant maintenance fees made owning an air conditioner even more costly.

NEXT

3:09   for the next 4 questions

PASSAGE

When I was growing up, I often got into a lot of trouble because of one of my habits. I would open all the windows in my room when it was hot in the summer. It was dangerous because we lived on the first floor, so my mom would be worried about my safety. Still, it did cool down our home and saved us money on electricity. Now, as an adult, I'm finally going to buy an air conditioner. I know it will be expensive, especially in the hot summer months. However, since I have children of my own now, I need to make sure that they're comfortable and safe.

Click and drag text to highlight the answer to the question below.

What was the author's mom worried about?

Highlight text in the passage to set an answer

NEXT

2:17   for the next 3 questions

PASSAGE

When I was growing up, I often got into a lot of trouble because of one of my habits. I would open all the windows in my room when it was hot in the summer. It was dangerous because we lived on the first floor, so my mom would be worried about my safety. Still, it did cool down our home and saved us money on electricity. Now, as an adult, I'm finally going to buy an air conditioner. I know it will be expensive, especially in the hot summer months. However, since I have children of my own now, I need to make sure that they're comfortable and safe.

Click and drag text to highlight the answer to the question below.

Why did the author get in trouble when he was growing up?

Highlight text in the passage to set an answer

NEXT

1:31   for the next 2 questions

PASSAGE

When I was growing up, I often got into a lot of trouble because of one of my habits. I would open all the windows in my room when it was hot in the summer. It was dangerous because we lived on the first floor, so my mom would be worried about my safety. Still, it did cool down our home and saved us money on electricity. Now, as an adult, I'm finally going to buy an air conditioner. I know it will be expensive, especially in the hot summer months. However, since I have children of my own now, I need to make sure that they're comfortable and safe.

Select the idea that is expressed in the passage.

○ I never had an air conditioner growing up, but now I can afford one for my family.

○ Opening windows lets a cool breeze pass quickly through your home.

○ When I'm looking for a new apartment, it's important whether it has air conditioning or not.

○ It's hard to stay in my house in the summer because I don't have air conditioning.

NEXT

1:03   for this question

PASSAGE

When I was growing up, I often got into a lot of trouble because of one of my habits. I would open all the windows in my room when it was hot in the summer. It was dangerous because we lived on the first floor, so my mom would be worried about my safety. Still, it did cool down our home and saved us money on electricity. Now, as an adult, I'm finally going to buy an air conditioner. I know it will be expensive, especially in the hot summer months. However, since I have children of my own now, I need to make sure that they're comfortable and safe.

Select the best title for the passage.

- ○ Air Conditioning for Less
- ○ Alternatives for Air Conditioning
- ○ My First Air Conditioner

NEXT

8:00   for the next 6 questions

PASSAGE

An urban park is a section of open space that has been ① laid / created / let / given / set aside for recreational use or to ② love / attract / protect / keep / conservation the natural ecosystem. It is usually maintained ③ by / to / inside / beside / from the city government. It provides green space ④ toward / enjoy / and / for / people visitors, and the grass is kept short to limit insect pests and ⑤ reduce / provide / inside / trim / eating areas for picnics and sports. Common ⑥ ideas / seeing / enough / entertain / features of an urban park ⑦ with / use / make / include / for playgrounds, gardening ⑧ design / areas / stores / produce / tips, hiking trails, ⑨ jogging / vehicle / place / woods / animal tracks, sports facilities ⑩ for / from / as / like / because baseball fields and basketball courts, and public restrooms.

Select the best sentence to fill in the blank in the passage.

① Select a word	∨
② Select a word	∨
③ Select a word	∨
④ Select a word	∨
⑤ Select a word	∨
⑤ Select a word	∨
⑥ Select a word	∨
⑦ Select a word	∨
⑧ Select a word	∨
⑨ Select a word	∨
⑩ Select a word	∨

NEXT

4:49   for the next 5 questions

PASSAGE

An urban park is a section of open space that has been set aside for recreational use or to protect the natural ecosystem. It is usually maintained by the city government. It provides green space for visitors, and the grass is kept short to limit insect pests and provide areas for picnics and sports. Common features of an urban park include playgrounds, gardening areas, hiking trails, jogging tracks, sports facilities like baseball fields and basketball courts, and public restrooms.

_____

A special type of urban park is a botanical garden. They are smaller than other parks and are used to grow specific types of native plant species.

Select the best sentence to fill in the blank in the passage.

- ○ We enjoyed the natural setting, but the parking lot was too far away.

- ○ Most parks also contain some sort of water feature, such as a pond or lake.

- ○ Studies have shown the social benefits of residents having access to an urban park.

- ○ Central Park in New York City occupies an area of 840 acres.

NEXT

4:09 | for the next 4 questions

PASSAGE

An urban park is a section of open space that has been set aside for recreational use or to protect the natural ecosystem. It is usually maintained by the city government. It provides green space for visitors, and the grass is kept short to limit insect pests and provide areas for picnics and sports. Common features of an urban park include playgrounds, gardening areas, hiking trails, jogging tracks, sports facilities like baseball fields and basketball courts, and public restrooms. Most parks also contain some sort of water feature, such as a pond or lake. A special type of urban park is a botanical garden. They are smaller than other parks and are used to grow specific types of native plant species.

Click and drag text to highlight the answer to the question below.

What is the definition of an urban park?

> Highlight text in the passage to set an answer

NEXT

3:17   for the next 3 questions

PASSAGE

An urban park is a section of open space that has been set aside for recreational use or to protect the natural ecosystem. It is usually maintained by the city government. It provides green space for visitors, and the grass is kept short to limit insect pests and provide areas for picnics and sports. Common features of an urban park include playgrounds, gardening areas, hiking trails, jogging tracks, sports facilities like baseball fields and basketball courts, and public restrooms. Most parks also contain some sort of water feature, such as a pond or lake. A special type of urban park is a botanical garden. They are smaller than other parks and are used to grow specific types of native plant species.

Click and drag text to highlight the answer to the question below.

How are botanical gardens different from other parks?

> Highlight text in the passage to set an answer

NEXT

2:31 for the next 2 questions

PASSAGE

An urban park is a section of open space that has been set aside for recreational use or to protect the natural ecosystem. It is usually maintained by the city government. It provides green space for visitors, and the grass is kept short to limit insect pests and provide areas for picnics and sports. Common features of an urban park include playgrounds, gardening areas, hiking trails, jogging tracks, sports facilities like baseball fields and basketball courts, and public restrooms. Most parks also contain some sort of water feature, such as a pond or lake. A special type of urban park is a botanical garden. They are smaller than other parks and are used to grow specific types of native plant species.

Select the idea that is expressed in the passage.

- ○ Parks benefit the environment by providing clean air and water.

- ○ Parks contain a variety of entertaining facilities for visitors.

- ○ Parks provide everything needed for a healthy fitness routine.

- ○ Parks are difficult for city governments to maintain.

NEXT

1:33   for this question

PASSAGE

An urban park is a section of open space that has been set aside for recreational use or to protect the natural ecosystem. It is usually maintained by the city government. It provides green space for visitors, and the grass is kept short to limit insect pests and provide areas for picnics and sports. Common features of an urban park include playgrounds, gardening areas, hiking trails, jogging tracks, sports facilities like baseball fields and basketball courts, and public restrooms. Most parks also contain some sort of water feature, such as a pond or lake. A special type of urban park is a botanical garden. They are smaller than other parks and are used to grow specific types of native plant species.

Select the best title for the passage.

○ An Introduction to Urban Parks

○ Keep Pests Out of Our Parks

○ Navigating Hiking Trails at Parks

○ A Visitor's Guide to the Local Park

NEXT

0:15

Interactive Listening

This section will have 2 conversations. For each conversation, you will have 4 minutes to select 5-7 conversation turns and 75 seconds to write a summary.

NEXT

1

4:00   for the next 5 questions

You will participate in a conversation about the scenario below.

You have done well in your journalism class and want to gain some job experience. You approach your professor about providing a reference for a part-time summer job at a local newspaper, and they agree to write one for you.

START

1-1

3:30   for the next 5 questions

Listen closely! You can only play the audio clips once.

🔊 AT(2)_10_1

Question 1 of 5
Select the best response.

○ Hi, Professor. I was wondering if I could see the class schedule.

○ Yes, actually. I'd be happy to lend a hand.

○ Hi, Professor. I have a question about this morning's lecture.

○ Hi, Professor. I was hoping you could do me a favor.

○ Thanks, Professor. I'm really looking forward to it.

NEXT

3:00   for the next 4 questions

 Hi, can I help you with something?

Hi, Professor. I was hoping you could do me a favor.

AT(2)_10_2

Question 2 of 5

Select the best response.

- ○ Would you be willing to proofread my résumé? I'm applying for a few journalism jobs, and I want to make sure my résumé looks professional.

- ○ I'm looking for some information on potential career paths in the journalism industry. I'd like to find a job quite quickly after I graduate from your course.

- ○ Is there any chance that you could provide a recommendation letter for me? I'm trying to join the university's Journalism Society, and your support would help my application.

- ○ If you don't find it, I'd like you to read over the first draft of my journalism essay. I want to make sure I'm on the right track before I continue.

- ○ I was wondering if you'd be able to give me a reference for a job application at a newspaper. I've been doing well in your class, and I want some job experience.

NEXT

2:30   for the next 3 questions

 Of course! What can I do for you?

I was wondering if you'd be able to give me a reference for a job application at a newspaper. I've been doing well in your class, and I want some job experience.

AT(2)_10_3

Question 3 of 5

Select the best response.

- ○ No, the application is due at the start of next month, and I need a reference from one of my professors.

- ○ Well, the deadline for the application is this Friday, so I was hoping I could get it within the next couple of days.

- ○ Yes, that's a good idea. I'll add some more information to my application to make it really stand out.

- ○ The deadline is tomorrow, but I was hoping to get an extension on my current lease until next month.

- ○ Well, this is probably the fifth job application I've submitted over the past three months.

NEXT

2:00   for the next 2 questions

 I'd be happy to do that for you. When do you need it by?

Well, the deadline for the application is this Friday, so I was hoping I could get it within the next couple of days.

  ▶

🔊 AT(2)_10_4

Question 4 of 5

Select the best response.

○ Yeah, I feel that having two references might help my chances of getting the job.

○ That would be a great addition to my résumé. Thanks for pointing that out.

○ Yes, that part of the application could be improved. I'll try to revise it this evening.

○ No, it's a part-time position, so I'll only be working two evenings every week.

○ Actually, I need two, but I already asked my previous employer to help out as well.

NEXT

1:30   for this question

That's plenty of time. Do you only need one reference for the job application?

Actually, I need two, but I already asked my previous employer to help out as well.

▶

🔊 AT(2)_10_5

Question 5 of 5
Select the best response.

○ Great. I'll see you there, then!

○ That's the type of advice I was looking for. Thanks!

○ I already received it. Thanks so much!

○ Awesome! I'm pleased that you like it, too!

○ That would be perfect. I appreciate it, Professor!

NEXT

Great. Well, please e-mail me with all the details about the job, and I'll try to send the reference to you by e-mail by 5 P.M. tomorrow.

That would be perfect. I appreciate it, Professor!

The task is complete.

NEXT

1-6

1:15

Summarize the conversation you just had in 75 seconds.

Your response

NEXT

4:00   for the next 5 questions

You will participate in a conversation about the scenario below.

You are considering dropping out from your university course, and you are discussing it with your friend. You are concerned about several issues related to the course.

START

3:30   for the next 5 questions

Listen closely! You can only play the audio clips once.

◁)) AT(2)_11_1

Question 1 of 5
Select the best response.

○ Well, you'd better apply for that course quickly then.

○ Oh, I didn't realize that you had enrolled in a different course.

○ To be honest, I am thinking about quitting the course.

○ Yes, I've already decided which course I'll apply for.

○ Actually, my next class is at 9 tomorrow morning.

NEXT

3:00   for the next 4 questions

 Do you think everything is going well with our university course?

To be honest, I was thinking about quitting the course.

🔊 AT(2)_11_2

Question 2 of 5

Select the best response.

○ I know! Our second year was so much more enjoyable than our first year.

○ I got a poor score on my recent assignment, so I'm thinking Biology is not the course for me.

○ Well, you certainly deserve to get good grades after all the hard work you've put in this year.

○ Exactly! All of the extra time I spent in the library has really paid off.

○ In that case, I don't mind going over our lecture notes with you, if you think it would help.

NEXT

2:30   for the next 3 questions

 Really? But you're almost finished with your second year! Have your grades not been so good recently?

I got a poor score on my recent assignment, so I'm thinking Biology is not the course for me.

🔊 AT(2)_11_3

Question 3 of 5

Select the best response.

○ I've been studying for it every evening, so I'm confident that I'll pass it.

○ I totally disagree. Some of the questions on the test were incredibly easy.

○ I'm not sure, but I think I'll go traveling at the end of the term.

○ I think the test will cover various topics like genetics and cell structure.

○ Actually, I did pass that, but only just. And I was disappointed with the score.

NEXT

2:00　　for the next 2 questions

 Don't let one poor grade get you down. How did you do on the mid-term test we just had?

Actually, I did pass that, but only just. And I was disappointed with the score.

🔊 AT(2)_11_4

Question 4 of 5

Select the best response.

○ I have to admit, that was definitely the most interesting part of our assignment.

○ I suppose some of them are okay, but there's not as much lab work as I expected. It's mostly all lectures.

○ You can find the class schedule on the website, or I could send you a copy of it by e-mail.

○ I'm interested in a lot of different things, so I don't really mind what topic I choose for the essay.

○ That's not a bad suggestion. You're right, I should consider switching to a biology course instead.

NEXT

1:30 for this question

 But I thought you were really interested in biology. Are you not finding our classes interesting?

I suppose some of them are okay, but there's not as much lab work as I expected. It's mostly all lectures.

  ▶ ━━━━━━━━━━━━━━

🔊 AT(2)_11_5

Question 5 of 5

Select the best response.

○ It might be a good idea to study together. That way I can help you with any parts that you find difficult.

○ Precisely. The practical work is the thing that gives me the most problems, so I could really use your help.

○ That's a good point. I'll see if I feel more motivated once we start doing the proper experiments in class.

○ You've been studying for two years? Then it's no surprise you're so knowledgeable about biology.

○ Sure. I'll check with the office to see if it's possible to change to another course as soon as possible.

NEXT

1:00   for this question

I guess that's true so far, but don't forget that we are supposed to do a lot more practical work next semester. Why don't you just wait and see if you enjoy it? It would be a shame to throw away two years of studying.

That's a good point. I'll see if I feel more motivated once we start doing the proper experiments in class.

The task is complete.

NEXT

2-6

1:15

Summarize the conversation you just had in 75 seconds.

Your response

NEXT

0:15

Writing

This section will have 4 writing questions: 3 Write About the Photo and 1 Interactive Writing. It will take up to 11 minutes.

NEXT

1

1:00

Write a description of the image below for 1 minute.

Your response

NEXT

2

1:00

Write a description of the image below for 1 minute.

Your response

NEXT

1:00

Write a description of the image below for 1 minute.

Your response

NEXT

5:00

❶ Write about the topic below for 5 minutes. **❷ Write a follow-up response for 3 minutes.**

Some people believe that it is important for students to begin learning computer skills in elementary school. Others argue that teaching computer skills may take time away from more important subjects or that young kids will not yet have the skills needed to learn about computers. What do you think?

Your response

CONTINUE AFTER 3 MINUTES

3:00

✓ Write about the topic below for 5 minutes. **❷ Write a follow-up response for 3 minutes.**

Some people believe that it is important for students to begin learning computer skills in elementary school. Others argue that teaching computer skills may take time away from more important subjects or that young kids will not yet have the skills needed to learn about computers. What do you think?

How might increased screen time, due to learning about computers, impact elementary school students?

Your response

Your response

CONTINUE AFTER 1 MINUTE

0:15

Speaking

This section will have 4 speaking questions. For each question, you will have 20 seconds to prepare and 90 seconds to respond.

NEXT

1

0:20

Prepare to speak about the topic below.
You will have 90 seconds to speak.

Number of replays left: 2

RECORD NOW

1:30

Speak about the topic for 90 seconds.

Number of replays left: 0

 ● RECORDING...   YOU CAN CONTINUE AFTER 30 SECONDS

AT(2)_12

2

0:20

Prepare to speak about the image below.
You will have 90 seconds to speak.

RECORD NOW

1:30

Speak about the image below for 90 seconds.

● RECORDING... YOU CAN CONTINUE AFTER 30 SECONDS

3

0:20

Prepare to speak about the topic below.

You will have 90 seconds to speak.

Describe something that irritates you.

• Why does it irritate you?

• How do you react when someone does this?

• Do you think this irritates others as well?

RECORD NOW

1:30

Speak about the topic below for 90 seconds.

Describe something that irritates you.

• Why does it irritate you?

• How do you react when someone does this?

• Do you think this irritates others as well?

● RECORDING... YOU CAN CONTINUE AFTER 30 SECONDS

4

Prepare to speak about the topic below.
You will have 90 seconds to speak.

Number of replays left: 2

RECORD NOW

AT(2)_13

1:30

Speak about the topic for 90 seconds.

Number of replays left: 0

● RECORDING... YOU CAN CONTINUE AFTER 30 SECONDS

0:15

Writing & Speaking Sample

This section will have a writing question and a speaking question. These 2 questions will contribute to your score and will also be available to the institutions that receive your results.

NEXT

1

0:30

Prepare to write about the topic below.

You will have 5 minutes to write.

> Describe something that young people can do to help the environment. How would doing this improve your community? Why is it important for young people to do things that benefit the environment?

START

5:00

Write about the topic below for 5 minutes.

Describe something that young people can do to help the environment. How would doing this improve your community? Why is it important for young people to do things that benefit the environment?

Your response

YOU CAN CONTINUE AFTER 3 MINUTES

0:30

Prepare to speak about the topic below.

You will have 3 minutes to speak.

How important do you think it is for learning to be fun for students? Is it the most important thing, or are there other aspects of education that are more important?

START

3:00

Speak about the topic below for 3 minutes.

How important do you think it is for learning to be fun for students? Is it the most important thing, or are there other aspects of education that are more important?

● RECORDING...   YOU CAN SUBMIT AFTER 1 MINUTE

Actual Test (2)
Answers

SECTION Read and Select

1	YES
2	YES
3	YES
4	NO
5	NO
6	YES
7	NO
8	NO
9	NO
10	NO
11	NO
12	YES
13	YES
14	NO
15	YES
16	YES
17	NO
18	NO

어휘

screen 화면 open 열다 choose 고르다 giving 주는 nuisance 골칫거리, 성가심 primarily 주로 monetary 통화의, 화폐의 fraudulent 사기의

SECTION Fill in the Blanks

1 charm
그의 매력은 그를 그 그룹의 팬들에게 가장 큰 사랑을 받도록 만들었습니다.

2 marked
눈 위에 있는 그들의 발자국들은 그들이 숲을 지나간 길을 표시했습니다.

3 squarely
그녀는 그의 눈을 똑바로 바라보며 아주 사소한 것까지 모든 것을 들어달라고 부탁했습니다.

4 Perhaps
아마도 저는 안전지대에서 벗어나 연기에 대한 열정을 추구할 때가 된 것 같습니다.

5 cancel
정책의 실행 가능성을 평가하는 것은 정책을 취소할 필요를 피하기 위해 매우 중요합니다.

6 dearly
우리는 예전처럼 온라인 채팅을 자주 할 수 없으니, 저는 그들이 무척 그립습니다.

7 consultation
최종 프로젝트를 시작하기 전에 당신의 교수님과 상담을 예약하여 아이디어를 브레인스토밍하고 피드백을 받도록 하세요.

8 affecting
경제 호황이 중소기업의 성장에 영향을 미치는 문제들을 부각시키고 있습니다.

어휘

charm 매력 footstep 발자국 mark 표시하다 take a path 길을 가다, 길을 선택하다 squarely 똑바로, 정면으로 perhaps 아마도 step out of ~에서 벗어나다 comfort zone 안전지대, 편안함 pursue 추구하다 passion 열정 acting 연기 evaluate 평가하다 feasibility 타당성, 가능성 implement 시행하다, 실행하다 policy 정책 crucial 중요한 avoid 피하다 cancel 취소하다 frequently 자주 used to ~하곤 했다 miss 그리워하다 dearly 무척, 몹시 schedule 일정을 잡다, 예약하다 consultation 상담 brainstorm 브레인스톰하다 boom 호황 highlight 부각시키다 affecting 영향을 미치는 growth 성장 small business 중소기업

Mixed Language Skills

1
I think I sat on it.
그 위에 앉았던 것 같아요.

2
저는 계속 수업에 참석하고 싶습니다.

3
It could be due to nausea or any number of things.
그것은 메스꺼움이나 어떤 여러가지 이유로 인한 것일 수 있습니다.

4
초창기의 정착민들은 연안 해역에서 얻을 수 있었던 풍부한 해산물을 이용했습니다.

5
The Millennium Bridge is a footbridge across the River Thames in London. It is a steel suspension bridge which links Bankside with the city. Its position is between Southwark Bridge (downstream) and Blackfriars Railway Bridge (upstream). The bridge opened on 10 June 2000. It is the newest bridge across the Thames.
밀레니엄 브리지는 런던의 템즈강을 가로지르는 보행자 전용 다리입니다. 그것은 뱅크사이드와 런던 시를 연결하는 강철 현수교입니다. 그것의 위치는 서더크 브리지(하류)와 블랙프라이어스 철도교(상류) 사이에 있습니다. 다리는 2000년 6월 10일에 개통되었습니다. 그것은 템즈강을 가로지르는 가장 최신의 다리입니다.

6
It dissolves in water to make an acidic solution of arsenious acid.
그것은 물에 용해되어 아비산의 산성 용액을 만듭니다.

7
그 책은 각기 다른 등장인물을 그린 여러 장의 서로 다른 앞표지들과 함께 출판되었습니다.

8
I will tell you about the winter event.
겨울 행사에 대해서 말씀드리겠습니다.

9
다음 주에 전기 기사가 와서 전선을 고칠 것입니다.

10
But the damage to hydrogen's reputation as a lifting gas was already done.
그러나 공기보다 가벼운 기체(리프팅 가스)로서의 수소의 평판은 이미 손상되었습니다.

11
Comet Leonard was discovered by astronomer Gregory J. Leonard on January 3 at the Mount Lemmon Observatory. The observatory is located on Mount Lemmon in the Santa Catalina Mountains, approximately 25 kilometers northeast of Tucson, Arizona. When Mr. Leonard found the comet's image, it was a faint object of magnitude 19. That is nearly 160,000 times dimmer than the faintest stars visible to the unaided eye. However, there is a chance that the comet will be seen clearly at its nearest point to Earth.
레너드 혜성은 1월 3일 레먼산 관측소에서 천문학자 그레고리 J. 레너드에 의해 발견되었습니다. 관측소는 애리조나 주 투싼시에서 북동쪽으로 약 25km 떨어진 산타카탈리나산맥의 레먼산에 위치하고 있습니다.

레너드 씨가 혜성의 이미지를 발견했을 때, 그것은 광도 19등급의 희미한 물체였습니다. 그것은 육안으로 볼 수 있는 가장 희미한 별들보다 거의 160,000배 더 어두운 것입니다. 그러나 지구와 가장 가까운 지점에서 그 혜성은 선명히 보일 가능성이 있습니다.

12 Some fish filter organic matter from the seawater.
일부 물고기들은 바닷물에서 유기물을 걸러냅니다.

13 사람들은 보통 중요하거나 돈이 많이 드는 일이 수행될 때 계약을 맺습니다.

14 The human voice is produced by the larynx.
사람의 목소리는 후두에서 만들어집니다.

15 Gregory: What is included in the meal special?
Waiter: If you order a large pasta, you'll get a salad and drink for free.
Gregory: I'll take the pasta, but can you tell the cook to add olives, please?
Waiter: Unfortunately, you can't add anything to the pasta and still get the free stuff.

그레고리: 특별 세트 메뉴에는 무엇이 포함되어 있나요?
웨이터: 라지 사이즈 파스타를 주문하시면 샐러드와 음료가 무료로 제공됩니다.
그레고리: 파스타로 주문할게요. 그런데 요리사에게 올리브를 추가해달라고 말씀해 주실 수 있나요?
웨이터: 아쉽게도 파스타에 무언가를 추가하면 무료 서비스 세트를 받는 것은 불가능합니다.

16 There are more than one hundred species of mammals here.
이곳에는 100종이 넘는 포유류가 있습니다.

17 맥주를 만드는 과정을 양조라고 합니다.

18 The study of metal alloys is a large part of material science.
금속 합금에 대한 연구는 재료 과학의 큰 부분을 차지합니다.

어휘

keep -ing 계속 ~하다 attend 출석하다, 다니다 early 초창기의 settler 정착민 take advantage of ~을 이용하다 abundance 풍부 seafood 해산물 access 접근, 이용 coastal waters 연안 해역 footbridge 보행자 전용 다리 suspension bridge 현수교 link 연결하다 position 위치 downstream (강의) 하류 upstream (강의) 상류 dissolve 녹다, 용해되다 acidic solution 산성 용액 arsenious acid 아비산 publish 출판하다 front cover 앞표지 depict 그리다, 묘사하다 character 등장인물 event 행사 electrician 전기 기사 fix 고치다 cable 전선 damage 손상 hydrogen 수소 reputation 평판, 명성 lifting gas 공기보다 가벼운 기체 comet 혜성 discover 발견하다 astronomer 천문학자 observatory 관측소 be located 위치하다 approximately 대략 faint 희미한 object 물체 magnitude (별의) 광도 dim 어두운 visible 보이는 unaided eye 육안 clearly 밝게, 또렷하게 filter 거르다 organic matter 유기물 seawater 바닷물 sign 서명하다 contract 계약 costly 많은 돈이 드는 produce 만들다 larynx 후두 include 포함하다 meal special 특별 세트 메뉴 for free 무료로 unfortunately 유감스럽게도 species 종 mammal 포유류 process 과정 beer 맥주 brewing 양조 metal alloy 금속 합금 material science 재료 과학

Interactive Reading

저는 자라면서 제 습관 중 하나 때문에 종종 많은 곤란에 빠졌습니다. 저는 여름에 더울 때 제 방의 모든 창문들을 열곤 했습 니다. 저희가 일층에 살기 때문에 위험해서 어머니는 제 안전을 걱정하시곤 했습니다. 하지만 그것은 우리 집을 시원하게 해서 우리는 전기 비용을 절약했습니다. 이제 성인이 되어서 드디어 에어컨을 사려고 합니다. 특히 더운 여름 날에는 비싼 것이라는 사실을 저는 알고 있습니다. 하지만 저는 지금 제 아이들이 있기 때문에 아이들이 편안하고 안전하도록 해야 합니다.

1-1 ① got ② lot ③ habits ④ be ⑤ it

1-2 (1) 저희 집은 계절에 상관없이 항상 추운 것 같습니다.
(2) **특히 더운 여름 날에는 비싸다는 것을 저는 알고 있습니다.**
(3) 제 남동생이 이 에어컨을 추천한 이유는 그의 집에서 너무 잘 작동하기 때문입니다.
(4) 지속적인 유지 관리 비용은 에어컨을 소유하는 것을 훨씬 더 비싸게 만들었습니다.

1-3 *저자의 어머니는 무엇을 걱정했습니까?*

my mom would be worried about my safety.

1-4 *왜 저자는 자라면서 곤란에 처했습니까?*

I would open all the windows in my room when it was hot in the summer.

1-5 (1) 저는 자라면서 에어컨을 가져본 적이 없지만 지금은 가족을 위해 하나 장만할 여유가 있습니다.
(2) 창문을 여는 것은 시원한 바람이 집 안을 빠르게 지나가게 합니다.
(3) 제가 새 아파트를 구할 때 에어컨이 있는지 없는지가 중요합니다.
(4) 에어컨이 없어서 여름에 제 집에 있기가 힘듭니다.

1-6 (1) 적은 비용으로 에어컨 키기
(2) 에어컨 키는 것에 대한 대안
(3) 나의 첫 에어컨

어휘

grow up 자라다, 성장하다 **get into trouble** 문제를 일으키다, 곤란에 처하다 **habit** 습관 **would** ~하곤 했다(과거에 자주 있었던 일에 대해 말할 때 사용) **safety** 안전 **cool down** 식히다 **air conditioner** 에어컨 **unit** 구성 단위 (예: 에어컨 한 대, 공동주택 한 가구)

도시 공원은 레크리에이션 용도로 또는 자연 생태계를 보호하기 위해 따로 마련된 개방된 공간의 한 부분입니다. 그것은 보통 시 정부에 의해 유지됩니다. 도시 공원은 방문객들에게 열린 공간을 제공하고, 잔디는 해충을 제한하고 소풍과 스포츠를 위한 공간을 제공하기 위해 짧게 유지됩니다. 도시 공원의 일반적인 특징은 놀이터, 정원 가꾸기 지역, 하이킹 코스, 조깅 트랙, 야구장과 농구장 같은 스포츠 시설, 그리고 공중 화장실을 포함합니다. 대부분의 공원들은 연못이나 호수 같은 물의 특징을 가지고 있습니다. 도시 공원의 특별한 유형은 식물원입니다. 식물원들은 다른 공원들보다 작고 특정한 종류의 토종 식물 종들을 기르기 위해 사용됩니다.

2-1 ① set ② protect ③ by ④ for ⑤ provide ⑥ features ⑦ include ⑧ areas ⑨ jogging ⑩ like

2-2 (1) 우리는 자연환경을 즐겼지만, 주차장이 너무 멀었습니다.
(2) 대부분의 공원들은 연못이나 호수 같은 물의 특징을 가지고 있습니다.
(3) 연구들은 도시 공원의 접근성을 가진 거주자들의 사회적 편익을 나타냅니다.
(4) 뉴욕의 센트럴 파크는 840 에이커의 면적을 차지하고 있습니다.

2-3 *도시 공원의 정의는 무엇입니까?*

An urban park is a section of open space that has been set aside for recreational use or to protect the natural ecosystem.

2-4 *식물원은 다른 공원과 어떻게 다릅니까?*

They are smaller than other parks and are used to grow specific types of native plant species.

2-5 (1) 공원은 깨끗한 공기와 물을 제공함으로써 환경에 이로움을 줍니다.
(2) 공원에는 방문객들을 위한 다양한·오락 시설이 있습니다.
(3) 공원은 건강한 운동 일과에 필요한 모든 것을 제공합니다.
(4) 공원은 시 정부가 유지하기 어렵습니다.

2-6 (1) 도시 공원 소개
(2) 해충이 우리 공원에 들어오지 못하게 하기
(3) 공원에서 하이킹 코스를 탐색하기
(4) 지역 공원으로의 방문객 안내

어휘

urban park 도시 공원 **section** 부분 **open space** 열린 공간, 공터 **set aside** 따로 놓아두다 **recreational** 레크리에이션의, 오락의 **natural ecosystem** 자연 생태계 **maintain** 유지하다 **city government** 시 정부 **provide A for B** B에게 A를 제공하다 **green space** 녹지 공간 **limit** 제한하다 **insect pest** 해충 **feature** 특징 **gardening** 정원 가꾸기 **hiking trail** 하이킹 코스 **sports facility** 스포츠 시설 **public restroom** 공중 화장실 **pond** 못, 연못 **social benefit** 사회적 이익 **resident** 거주자 **botanical garden** 식물원 **native** 토종의 **species** 종

당신은 아래 주제에 대한 대화에 참여하게 됩니다.

당신은 저널리즘 수업에서 좋은 성적을 거두고 있으며 직무 경험을 쌓고 싶어합니다. 지역 신문사에서 여름 기간 동안 아르바이트를 하기 위해 교수님께 추천서에 대하여 문의하였고, 교수님은 써주는 것에 동의합니다.

(음원) 안녕하세요, 무엇을 도와드릴까요?

1-1
(1) 교수님 안녕하세요. 수업 일정을 볼 수 있을까 해서요.
(2) 네, 그렇습니다. 기꺼이 도와드리겠습니다.
(3) 교수님 안녕하세요. 오늘 아침 강의에 대해 질문이 있습니다.
(4) 교수님 안녕하세요. 부탁 하나 들어주셨으면 해서요.
(5) 감사합니다, 교수님. 정말 기대가 됩니다.

(음원) 그럼요! 무엇을 도와드릴까요?

1-2
(1) 제 이력서를 교정해 주실 수 있나요? 몇 개의 저널리즘 직무에 지원하고 있는데, 제 이력서가 전문성 있게 보이는지 확인 하고 싶습니다.
(2) 저널리즘계에 잠재적인 경로에 대한 커리어 정보를 찾고 있습니다. 이 수업을 이수한 후 빨리 취직하고 싶습니다.
(3) 혹시 저에게 추천서를 제공해 주실 수 있나요? 대학 저널리즘 학회에 가입하려고 하는데, 지원서에 교수님의 지원이 도움이 될 것입니다.
(4) 찾지 못할 경우, 제 저널리즘 에세이의 초고를 읽어주셨으면 합니다. 계속하기 전에 제가 올바른 방향으로 가고 있는지 확인하고 싶습니다.
(5) 신문사 직무 지원을 위한 추천서를 제공해 주실 수 있는지 궁금합니다. 교수님의 저널리즘 수업에서 좋은 성적을 거두고 있으며, 직무 경험을 쌓고 싶습니다.

(음원) 기꺼이 그렇게 해드리겠습니다. 언제까지 필요하신가요?

1-3
(1) 아니요, 지원서 제출은 다음달 초에 마감이며, 교수님 중 한 명의 추천서가 필요합니다.
(2) 음, 지원 마감일이 이번 주 금요일이라서 며칠 내로 받을 수 있기를 바랐습니다.
(3) 네, 좋은 생각입니다. 지원서에 몇 가지 정보를 더 추가하여 정말 돋보이게 만들겠습니다.
(4) 마감일이 내일이지만, 현재 임대 계약을 다음 달까지 연장하고 싶습니다.
(5) 지난 3개월 동안 제출한 입사 지원서가 이번이 다섯 번째입니다.

(음원) 충분한 시간이네요. 입사 지원 시 추천인이 한 명만 필요하나요?

1-4
(1) 네, 추천인이 두 명 있으면 취업에 도움이 될 것 같습니다.
(2) 이력서에 추가하면 정말 좋을 것 같습니다. 지적해 주셔서 감사합니다.
(3) 네, 지원서에 해당 부분이 개선될 수 있습니다. 오늘 저녁에 수정해 보겠습니다.
(4) 아니요, 아르바이트라서, 매주 저녁 2번만 근무할 것입니다.
(5) 사실, 두 명이 필요하지만, 이전 고용주에게도 이미 도움을 요청했습니다.

(음원) 잘됐네요. 그럼 직무에 대한 모든 세부 정보를 이메일로 보내주시면 내일 오후 5시까지 추천서를 보내드리도록 하겠습니다.

1-5
(1) 좋아요. 그럼 거기서 뵙겠습니다!
(2) 제가 찾던 조언이 바로 그거였어요. 감사합니다!
(3) 이미 받았습니다. 정말 감사합니다!
(4) 아주 좋습니다! 마음에 드신다니 정말 기쁘네요!
(5) 그럼 완벽하겠네요. 감사합니다, 교수님!

1-6
I was speaking with my professor because I wanted her to provide a reference for a job I am applying for. She said she would be happy to help me. She checked when I would need the reference by and whether I only need one. In the end, she asked me to send some details by e-mail and promised to send the reference by 5 tomorrow.

나는 지원하는 일자리를 위한 추천서를 교수님께 받고 싶어서 교수님과 이야기했습니다. 교수님은 기꺼이 도와주신다고 말씀해 주셨습니다. 교수님은 언제까지 필요하고 추천인 한 명만 필요한지 확인하셨습니다. 결국, 직무에 대한 세부 정보를 이메일로 보내주는 것을 요구하셨고 내일 오후 5시까지 추천서를 보내주겠다고 약속하셨습니다.

모범답안 분석

도입부 내용 한 문장:	I was speaking with my professor because I wanted her to provide a reference for a job I am applying for.
대화 핵심 내용 두 문장:	She said she would be happy to help me. She checked when I would need the reference by and whether I only need one.
결론/마무리 한 문장:	In the end, she asked me to send some details by e-mail and promised to send the reference by 5 tomorrow.

어휘

be happy to 기꺼이 ~하다 favor 부탁 résumé 이력서 recommendation letter 추천서 application 지원(서)
reference 추천(인) deadline 마감일 lease 임대 계약 submit 제출하다 revise 수정하다 employer 고용주

당신은 아래 주제에 대한 대화에 참여하게 됩니다.

당신은 대학 과정을 중퇴하는 것을 고려하고 있으며 그에 대해 친구와 논의하고 있습니다.

당신은 수업과 관련된 몇 가지 문제에 대해 우려하고 있습니다.

(음원) 대학 과정이 잘 진행되고 있다고 생각해?

2-1　　(1) 그럼 그 강좌를 빨리 신청하는 것이 좋겠네.
　　　　　(2) 오, 다른 과정에 등록한 줄 몰랐어.
　　　　　(3) 솔직히, 과정을 그만둘까 생각하고 있어.
　　　　　(4) 응, 신청할 과정을 이미 결정했어.
　　　　　(5) 사실, 내 다음 수업은 내일 오전 9시에 있어.

(음원) 정말? 하지만 2학년을 거의 끝마쳤잖아! 최근 성적이 그다지 좋지 않았어?

2-2　　(1) 알아! 2학년이 1학년 보다 훨씬 즐거웠어.
　　　　　(2) 최근 과제에서 낮은 점수를 받았기 때문에, 생물학은 나에게 맞지 않는 과정이라고 생각해.
　　　　　(3) 뭐, 올해 열심히 노력한 만큼 좋은 성적을 받을 충분한 자격이 있어.
　　　　　(4) 그러니까! 내가 도서관에 보낸 모든 추가적인 시간에 대해 정말로 성과가 있었어.
　　　　　(5) 그렇다면, 너가 도움이 될 것 같다고 생각하면, 너와 함께 강의 노트를 살펴보는 것도 좋아.

(음원) 낮은 성적 하나가 실망시키게 하지 마. 최근에 치른 중간고사 시험은 어땠어?

2-3　　(1) 매일 저녁 공부를 해왔기 때문에 합격할 자신이 있어.
　　　　　(2) 난 전적으로 동의하지 않아. 시험 문제 중 일부는 엄청나게 쉬웠어.
　　　　　(3) 잘 모르겠지만, 학기가 끝나면 여행을 떠날 것 같아.
　　　　　(4) 시험은 유전학과 세포 구조와 같은 다양한 주제를 다룰 것 같아.
　　　　　(5) 사실, 통과는 했지만 겨우 통과했을 뿐이야. 그리고 점수에 실망했어.

(음원) 하지만 난 네가 생물학에 관심이 많다고 생각했어. 우리 수업이 흥미롭다고 생각하지 않아?

2-4　　(1) 인정할 수밖에 없어, 이번 과제에서 가장 흥미로웠던 부분이 바로 그거였어.
　　　　　(2) 일부는 괜찮지만, 기대한 것 보다 실험실 실습이 많지 않았어. 대부분이 다 강의야.
　　　　　(3) 수업 일정은 웹사이트에서 확인하거나, 이메일로 사본을 보내줄 수 있어.
　　　　　(4) 나는 다양한 것들에 관심이 많아서, 에세이 주제로 어떤 것을 선택하든 크게 신경 쓰지 않아.
　　　　　(5) 나쁘지 않은 제안이야. 맞아, 대신 생물학 과정으로 바꾸는 것을 고려해야겠어.

(음원) 지금까지는 그런 것 같아, 하지만 다음 학기에는 훨씬 더 많은 실습을 해야 한다는 것을 잊지 마. 이 과정을
　　　 좋아하는지 일단 기다려 보는 것은 어때? 2년 동안 공부한 것을 버리기에는 너무 아까워.

2-5　　(1) 같이 공부하는 것이 좋은 생각일 수 있어. 그렇게 하면 어려운 부분들에 대해 도와줄 수 있어.
　　　　　(2) 바로 그거야. 실무가 가장 문제를 주기 때문에, 정말 너의 도움이 필요해.
　　　　　(3) 좋은 지적이야. 수업에 제대로 된 실험을 시작하면 더 동기 부여가 될 수 있어.
　　　　　(4) 2년 동안 공부하고 있었어? 그렇다면 생물학에 대해 잘 알고 있는 것은 당연해.
　　　　　(5) 물론이지. 가능한 한 빨리 다른 과정으로 변경할 수 있는지 사무실에 확인해 볼게.

2-6　　I was talking with my friend about dropping out of the biology course I enrolled in. He
　　　　　thought it was a bad idea, but I was disappointed with my recent grades and the lack of
　　　　　practical work in the laboratory. He told me not to worry about the grades and reminded me

that we will do more lab work soon. In the end, I decided to wait and see how it goes.

나는 생물학 과정을 중퇴하는 것에 대해 친구와 이야기를 하고 있었습니다. 친구는 좋지 않은 생각이라고 생각했지만 나는 최근 성적과 실험실에서 실무 실습이 부족한 것에 대해 실망하고 있었습니다. 친구는 성적에 대해 걱정하지 말라고 이야기 했고 곧 더 많은 실험실 실습이 있을 것이라고 상기해줬습니다. 결국에, 나는 어떻게 진행되는지 기다려 보기로 결정했습니다.

모범답안 분석

도입부 내용 한 문장: I was talking with my friend about dropping out of the Biology course I enrolled in.

대화 핵심 내용 두 문장: He thought it was a bad idea, but I was disappointed with my recent grades and the lack of practical work in the laboratory. He told me not to worry about the grades and reminded me that we will do more lab work soon.

결론/마무리 한 문장: In the end, I decided to wait and see how it goes.

어휘

drop out 중퇴하다, 중간에 그만두다   pay off 성과가 있다   genetics 유전학   cell structure 세포 구조   copy 사본   mind 신경 쓰다   suggestion 제안   switch 바꾸다   wait and see 기다려 보다   practical work 실무 (실습)   experiment 실험   laboratory(=lab) 실험실

SECTION   Writing

1   This is a photograph of several people marching and wearing the same T-shirt. In detail, the people in the front are holding a banner, and the people behind them are holding flags from different countries.

이것은 여러 사람이 같은 티셔츠를 입고 행진하는 사진입니다. 자세히 보면 앞쪽의 사람들은 현수막을 들고 있고, 뒤쪽의 사람들은 다른 나라의 국기를 들고 있습니다.

2   This is a photograph of a man playing the guitar at a concert. In detail, he is dressed casually in a white long-sleeved T-shirt and jeans. In the left corner, there is a microphone, which shows that he could be a singer.

이것은 콘서트에서 기타를 연주하는 한 남자의 사진입니다. 자세히 보면 그는 흰색 긴팔 티셔츠와 청바지를 입고 캐주얼하게 차려입고 있습니다. 왼쪽 구석에는 마이크가 있어 그가 가수일 수 있음을 보여줍니다.

3   This is a photograph of a snowman with a frowning face. In detail, it is wearing a black hat made of plastic. On top of that, it looks like it is a warm day since the snowman has started to melt on the grass.

이것은 찡그린 얼굴을 한 눈사람의 사진입니다. 자세히 보면 플라스틱으로 만든 검은색 모자를 쓰고 있습니다. 게다가 눈사람이 잔디 위에서 녹기 시작했기 때문에 따뜻한 날인 것처럼 보입니다.

4 *① 어떤 사람들은 학생들이 초등학교 때부터 컴퓨터 기술을 배우는 것이 중요하다고 생각합니다. 다른 사람들은 컴퓨터 기술을 가르치느라 더 중요한 과목에 시간을 빼앗기거나 어린 아이들이 아직 컴퓨터를 배우는 데 필요한 기술을 갖추지 못할 것이라고 주장합니다. 여러분은 어떻게 생각합니까?*

In my perspective, it is more beneficial to teach elementary school students computer skills. The main reason is that doing so would promote digital literacy. In today's digital age, computers are being used in almost all aspects of life, including communication, education, and business. Thus, being proficient with computers at a young age will help them be better prepared for the future.

Additionally, computer skills are needed for schoolwork. For example, students may need to create presentation slides and documents for class assignments. Thus, it is better for children to start acquiring these skills as soon as possible. To conclude, I think that it is important for students to begin learning computer skills in elementary school.

제 생각에는 초등학생에게 컴퓨터 기술을 가르치는 것이 더 유익합니다. 가장 큰 이유는 그렇게 함으로써 디지털 리터러시를 촉진할 수 있기 때문입니다. 오늘날의 디지털 시대에는 컴퓨터가 커뮤니케이션, 교육, 비즈니스 등 거의 모든 생활 영역에서 사용되고 있습니다. 따라서 어릴 때부터 컴퓨터를 능숙하게 다룰 수 있으면 미래를 더 잘 준비할 수 있습니다.

또한 컴퓨터 기술은 학업에도 필요합니다. 예를 들어, 학생들은 수업 과제를 위해 프레젠테이션 슬라이드와 문서를 만들어야 할 수도 있습니다. 따라서 아이들이 가능한 한 빨리 이러한 기술을 습득하기 시작하는 것이 좋습니다. 결론적으로 저는 학생들이 초등학교 때부터 컴퓨터 기술을 배우는 것이 중요하다고 생각합니다.

② 컴퓨터 학습으로 인한 스크린 타임 증가가 초등학생에게 어떤 영향을 미칠까요?

It is true that increased screen time can impact elementary school students negatively. Computers can be a source of distraction and cause eye strain. However, if schools control the amount of screen time students are exposed to, I believe the negative effects can be avoided.

증가된 화면 사용 시간이 초등학생에게 부정적인 영향을 미칠 수 있는 것은 사실입니다. 컴퓨터는 주의 산만의 근원이 될 수 있고 눈의 피로를 야기할 수 있습니다. 하지만 학교에서 학생들이 스크린에 노출되는 시간을 통제한다면 부정적인 영향은 피할 수 있다고 생각합니다.

어휘

march 행진하다 banner 현수막 flag 국기 guitar 기타 long-sleeved 긴팔의 jeans 청바지 microphone 마이크 frowning 찡그린 made of ~로 만들어진 melt 녹다 grass 잔디 beneficial 유익한 elementary school 초등학교 subject 과목 literacy 읽고 쓰는 능력 digital literacy 디지털 리터러시(디지털 정보 해독 능력) digital age 디지털 시대 aspect 영역, 면 proficient 능숙한 better prepared 더 잘 준비된 schoolwork 학업 assignment 과제 acquire 습득하다 screen time 스크린 타임(화면 사용 시간) source 근원 distraction 주의 산만 cause 야기하다 eye strain 눈의 피로 expose 노출하다

SECTION Speaking

1 *Talk about a famous person you would like to meet before you die. What is this person famous for, and why do you want to meet this person?*
죽기 전에 만나고 싶은 유명한 사람에 대해 이야기해 보세요. 이 사람은 무엇으로 유명하며 왜 그 사람을 만나고 싶습니까?

One famous person I would like to meet is the sports star, Son Heung-min. He is a professional soccer player who gained global recognition for his exceptional performance on the field. He is also well known for playing for Tottenham Hotspur, one of the most famous soccer teams, and the South Korean national team. As someone who is passionate about soccer, I am proud to see him represent my country internationally. I would love to meet him in person and have a conversation with him about his journey to success. For these reasons, Son Heung-min is the person I would like to meet before I die.

제가 만나고 싶은 유명인 중 한 명은 스포츠 스타 손흥민 선수입니다. 그는 경기장에서 뛰어난 활약으로 전 세계적인 인정을 받는 프로 축구 선수입니다. 그는 가장 유명한 축구팀 중 하나인 토트넘 핫스퍼와 대한민국 국가대표팀에서 뛰는 것으로도 잘 알려져 있습니다. 축구에 대한 열정을 가진 사람으로서 그가 국제적으로 한국을 대표하게 되어 자랑스럽습니다. 손흥민 선수를 직접 만나 성공의 여정에 대해 이야기를 나누고 싶습니다. 이런 이유로 손흥민 선수는 제가 죽기 전에 꼭 만나고 싶은 사람입니다.

2 This is a picture of a young child holding his mother's hand. In detail, I can see that they are walking through a tunnel. On top of that, the mother is holding a bag. From this, I can infer that they have been shopping for some groceries. And in the background, there is a wall with some graffiti on it. This clearly shows that they are in the city.

이것은 엄마의 손을 잡고 있는 어린 아이의 사진입니다. 자세히 보면, 터널을 지나고 있는 것을 볼 수 있습니다. 그 위에 어머니는 가방을 들고 있습니다. 이를 통해 식료품을 사러 간 것으로 유추할 수 있습니다. 그리고 배경에는, 그래피티가 그려진 벽이 있습니다. 이것은 그들이 도시에 있다는 것을 분명히 보여줍니다.

3   *당신을 짜증나게 하는 것에 대해 설명하십시오.*
  · 왜 그것이 당신을 짜증나게 합니까?
  · 누군가가 이것을 할 때 당신은 어떻게 대응합니까?
  · 다른 사람들도 이것으로 짜증이 난다고 생각합니까?

One thing that irritates me is when someone repeats the same words over and over again. The main reason why this annoys me is because it is a waste of time for me to listen to the same thing again. When someone does this, I usually react by interrupting them or cutting them off when they are talking. This might sound a little rude, but the important point is telling them that they are being repetitive very politely. Personally, I think that this would irritate others as well. Not many people would enjoy listening to the same thing again and again.

저를 짜증나게 하는 것 중 하나는 누군가가 같은 말을 계속 반복할 때입니다. 이것이 짜증나는 가장 큰 이유는 같은 말을 다시 듣는 것이 시간 낭비이기 때문입니다. 누군가가 이런 행동을 하면 저는 보통 말을 끊거나 상대방의 말을 자르는 방식으로 대응합니다. 약간 무례하게 들릴 수도 있지만, 중요한 점은 상대방이 반복적으로 말하고 있다는 것을 매우 정중하게 말하는 것입니다. 개인적으로 이런 행동은 다른 사람에게도 짜증을 유발할 수 있다고 생각합니다. 같은 말을 반복해서 듣는 것을 좋아하는 사람은 많지 않을 테니까요.

4   *Discuss the ways the government and organizations in your country conserve the environment.*
당신 나라의 정부와 단체가 환경을 보호하는 방법에 대해 논하십시오.

There are many different ways that the government and organizations conserve the environment, but the first way that comes to mind is encouraging the use of bicycles to commute. These days, many people go to work or school by car. However, because the government promotes riding bicycles by providing affordable bike services, more people are using them, resulting in less pollution. Another way is placing more trash cans in public places. That way, people are throwing away their trash properly instead of littering. In conclusion, encouraging the use of bicycles and placing more trash cans is helpful in preserving the environment.

정부와 단체가 환경을 보호하는 방법에는 여러 가지가 있지만, 가장 먼저 떠오르는 것은 출퇴근 시 자전거 이용을 장려하는 것입니다. 요즘에는 많은 사람들이 자동차로 직장이나 학교에 통학합니다. 하지만 정부가 저렴한 자전거 서비스를 제공하여 자전거 타기를 장려하면서 더 많은 사람들이 자전거를 이용하고 있고, 그 결과 공해가 줄어들고 있습니다. 또 다른 방법은 공공장소에 쓰레기통을 더 많이 배치하는 것입니다. 이렇게 하면 사람들이 쓰레기를 함부로 버리지 않고 제대로 버리게 됩니다. 결론적으로, 자전거 이용을 장려하고 쓰레기통을 더 많이 배치하는 것이 환경 보호에 도움이 됩니다.

Actual Test (2)
Answers

어휘

professional soccer player 프로 축구 선수 global recognition 세계적인 인정 exceptional performance 뛰어난 활약 on the field 경기장에서 national team 국가대표팀 passionate 열정적인 represent 대표하다 internationally 국제적으로 in person 직접 journey to success 성공으로의 여정 hold 잡다 tunnel 터널 infer 유추하다 groceries 식료품 graffiti 그래피티 irritate 짜증나게 하다 waste of time 시간 낭비 react 대응하다, 반응하다 interrupt 가로막다 cut off 끊다 rude 무례한 repetitive 되풀이하는 politely 정중하게 personally 개인적으로 organization 단체 conserve 보호하다 come to mind 생각이 떠오르다 encourage 장려하다 commute 통근하다 promote 홍보하다 provide 제공하다 affordable 저렴한 pollution 오염 place 배치하다 trash can 쓰레기통 throw away 버리다 properly 제대로 litter 쓰레기 등을 버려 어지럽히다

SECTION | Writing & Speaking Sample

1 젊은이들이 환경을 돕기 위해 할 수 있는 것을 설명하십시오. 이를 통해 공동체를 어떻게 개선할 수 있습니까? 젊은이들이 환경에 도움되는 일을 하는 것이 왜 중요합니까?

There are several things that young people can do to preserve the environment. However, in my view, minimizing the use of plastic is the most effective way. The issue with plastic waste is that it is not biodegradable. If young people reduce the use of plastic by using personal water bottles instead of plastic cups, there would be less plastic waste that may ruin the environment. Another way young people can help the environment is planting trees. By doing so, it can provide shelter and food for many birds. It is especially important for youth to do things for the environment. If they learn to preserve the environment when they are young, they can bring about positive effects for the environment for the rest of their lives.

젊은이들이 환경을 보존하기 위해 할 수 있는 몇 가지 일들이 있습니다. 하지만, 제가 보기에, 플라스틱 사용을 최소화하는 것이 가장 효과적인 방법입니다. 플라스틱 쓰레기의 문제는 그것이 생분해되지 않는다는 것입니다. 만약 젊은이들이 플라스틱 컵 대신 개인 물병을 사용함으로써 플라스틱 사용을 줄인다면, 환경을 파괴할 수 있는 플라스틱 쓰레기가 줄어들 것입니 다. 젊은이들이 환경을 도울 수 있는 또 다른 방법은 나무를 심는 것입니다. 그렇게 함으로써, 그것은 많은 새들에게 은신처와 먹이를 제공할 수 있습니다. 젊은이들은 환경을 위해 무언가를 하는 것이 특히 중요합니다. 만약 그들이 어렸을 때 환경을 보존하는 법을 배운다면, 그들은 남은 인생 동안 환경에 긍정적인 효과를 가져올 수 있습니다.

2 학생들에게 재미를 주는 학습이 얼마나 중요하다고 생각하십니까? 그것이 가장 중요한 것입니까, 아니면 더 중요한 교육의 다른 측면이 있습니까?

Of course, people might have different opinions on this, but I think that learning should be fun for students to some extent. This is because if students are interested in learning itself, it can be a natural motivator for them to study harder. On the other hand, if learning is boring, it is unlikely that students would endure their education. However, I think that it should not be the most important thing when it comes to education. The quality of education the students get should be the most crucial factor. This can include the teachers, the curriculum, and the subjects they learn. To conclude, there are many aspects that can be important when learning. However, in my view, the quality is the most important.

물론, 사람들은 이것에 대해 다른 의견을 가지고 있을 수 있지만, 저는 배우는 것이 학생들에게 어느 정도 재미있어야 한다고 생각합니다. 학생들이 학습 자체에 관심이 있다면 그들이 더 열심히 공부할 수 있는 자연스러운 동기부여가 될 수 있기 때문 입니다. 반면에, 만약 배움이 지루하다면, 학생들이 그들의 교육을 견디기 어려울 것입니다. 하지만, 저는 그것이 교육에 있어서 가장 중요한 것이 되어서는 안 된다고 생각합니다. 학생들이 받는 교육의 질이 가장 중요한 요소가 되어야 합니다. 여기에는 교사, 커리큘럼, 그리고 그들이 배우는 과목이 포함될 수 있습니다. 결론적으로, 배울 때 중요할 수 있는 많은 측면이 있습니다. 하지만 제 생각에는 교육의 질이 가장 중요합니다.

어휘

environment 환경 improve 개선하다 community 지역 사회, 공동체 benefit 이익이 되다, 유익하다 preserve 지키다, 보호하다 minimize 최소화하다 effective 효과적인 issue 문제 plastic waste 플라스틱 폐기물 biodegradable 생분해성의, 자연분해성의 reduce 줄이다, 낮추다 water bottle 물병 ruin 망치다, 폐허로 만들다 plant trees 나무를 심다 shelter 은신처, 주거지 bring about ~을 유발하다 positive effect 긍정적 영향, 긍정적 효과 the rest of ~의 나머지 aspect 측면 to some extent 다소, 어느 정도까지 motivator 동기를 부여하는 것[사람] on the other hand 다른 한편으로는, 반면에 endure 견디다, 참다 when it comes to ~에 있어서는, ~에 관해서라면 quality of education 교육의 질 crucial 중대한, 결정적인 factor 요인 curriculum 교육과정 subject 과목, 주제 conclude 결론을 내리다, 끝내다

실전문제

3

Actual Test (3)

0:15

Read and Select

This section will have 15-18 questions. For each question, you will see a word on the screen. You will have 5 seconds to decide if the word is a real word in English.

NEXT

1

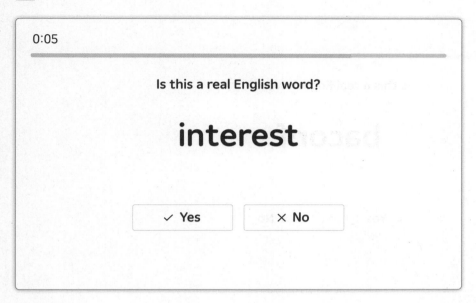

0:05

Is this a real English word?

interest

✓ Yes   ✕ No

2

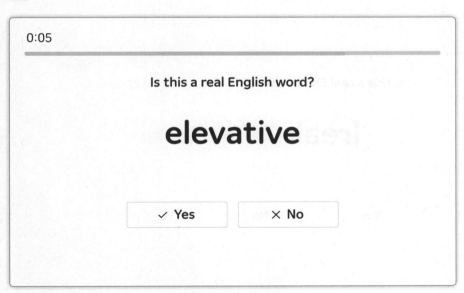

0:05

Is this a real English word?

elevative

✓ Yes   ✕ No

3

0:05

Is this a real English word?

baconf

✓ Yes   ✕ No

4

0:05

Is this a real English word?

lreak

✓ Yes   ✕ No

5

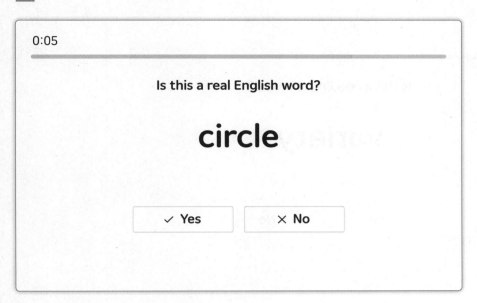

0:05

Is this a real English word?

circle

✓ Yes   ✕ No

6

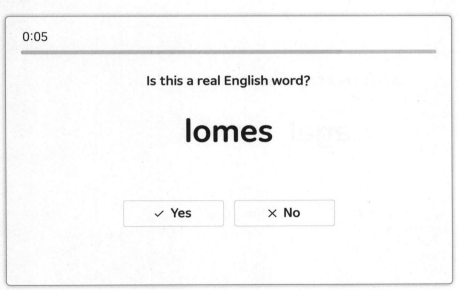

0:05

Is this a real English word?

lomes

✓ Yes   ✕ No

7

8

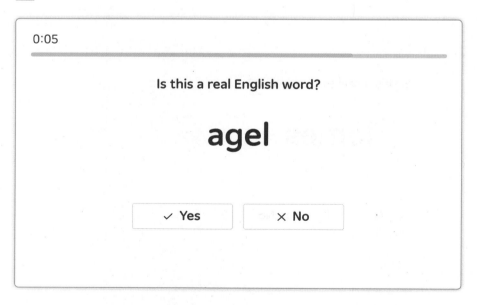

9

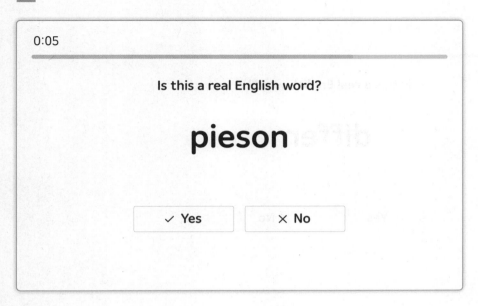

0:05

Is this a real English word?

pieson

✓ Yes   ✕ No

10

0:05

Is this a real English word?

methin

✓ Yes   ✕ No

11

0:05

Is this a real English word?

differ

✓ Yes   ✕ No

12

0:05

Is this a real English word?

afraid

✓ Yes   ✕ No

13

0:05

Is this a real English word?

easily

✓ Yes   ✕ No

14

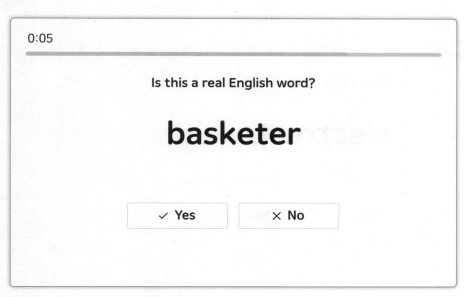

0:05

Is this a real English word?

basketer

✓ Yes   ✕ No

0:05

Is this a real English word?

office

✓ Yes   × No

0:05

Is this a real English word?

electrest

✓ Yes   × No

17

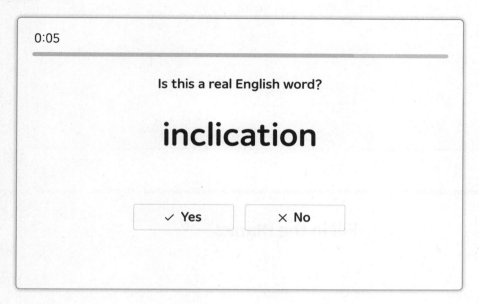

0:05

Is this a real English word?

inclication

✓ Yes   ✕ No

18

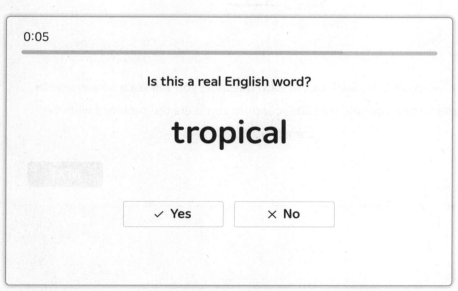

0:05

Is this a real English word?

tropical

✓ Yes   ✕ No

0:15

Fill in the Blanks

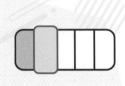

This section will have 6-9 questions. For each question, you will see a sentence with an unfinished word. You will have 20 seconds to complete the sentence with the correct word.

NEXT

1

0:20

Complete the sentence with the correct word.

Even though I wanted to `s` `t` `☐` talking, I found myself continuing the conversation out of politeness.

NEXT

2

0:20

Complete the sentence with the correct word.

In order to easily memorize the students' names, the professor instituted the use of a `s` `e` `a` `☐` `☐` `☐` chart.

NEXT

3

0:20

Complete the sentence with the correct word.

When Kevin received news of his promotion, he couldn't help

`c` `r` `y` `☐` `☐` tears of joy.

NEXT

4

0:20

Complete the sentence with the correct word.

Located on the edge of town, the quaint coffee shop was her favorite

weekend `g` `e` `t` `☐` `☐` spot.

NEXT

5

0:20

Complete the sentence with the correct word.

Can you send me the video c | l   of us dancing at the wedding?

NEXT

6

0:20

Complete the sentence with the correct word.

Your first promotion is a major m | i | l | e   .

NEXT

7

0:20

Complete the sentence with the correct word.

The pitcher watched as the hitter skillfully | b | a | t | | | the baseball across the field.

NEXT

8

0:20

Complete the sentence with the correct word.

After a long jog in the hot sun, my clothes felt incredibly | s | w | e | | | and dirty.

NEXT

0:20

Complete the sentence with the correct word.

Did you know that our subdivision takes up almost half a square m i ☐ ?

NEXT

Mixed Language Skills

This section will have 18-21 questions from three question types: Read and Complete, Listen and Type, and Read Aloud. It will take up to 30 minutes.

NEXT

1

1:00

_____

Type the statement that you hear.

Your response

Number of replays left: 2

🔊 AT(3)_1

NEXT

2

0:20

_____

Record yourself saying the statement below.

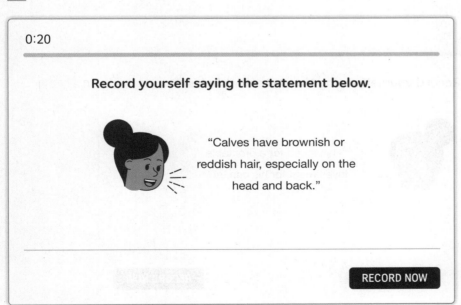

"Calves have brownish or reddish hair, especially on the head and back."

RECORD NOW

3

1:00

Type the statement that you hear.

> Your response

Number of replays left: 2

NEXT

4

0:20

Record yourself saying the statement below.

"He looked for a profitable investment for his capital."

RECORD NOW

5

3:00

Type the missing letters to complete the text below.

Political philosophy as a discipline addresses the nature, scope, and legitimacy of legal authority and how people interact with it. It `i`▢ sometimes `t h o`▢▢▢ of `a`▢ a `p a`▢ of `p o l i`▢▢▢▢ science. It `a s`▢ questions `s u`▢▢ as "What `i`▢ the `u l t i`▢▢▢▢ source `o`▢ justice?" and "How does a government maintain its authority?"

NEXT

6

1:00

Type the statement that you hear.

◁)) AT(3)_3

Your response

Number of replays left: 2

NEXT

7

> 0:20
>
> ---
>
> ### Record yourself saying the statement below.
>
>
>
> "As a result, state revenue has increased 14 times since the mid-1990s."
>
> ---
>
> RECORD NOW

8

> 1:00
>
> ---
>
> ### Type the statement that you hear.
>
>
>
> Your response
>
> Number of replays left: 2
>
> ---
>
> NEXT

AT(3)_4

9

0:20

Record yourself saying the statement below.

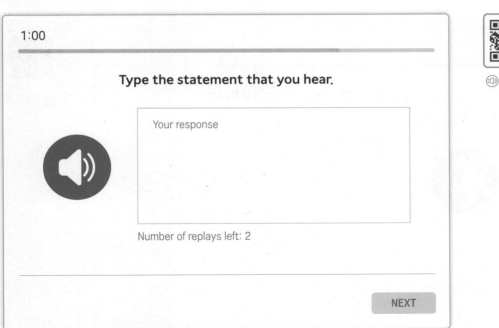

"These products are often sold in portion-controlled, single-serve packaging designed for portability."

RECORD NOW

10

1:00

Type the statement that you hear.

Your response

Number of replays left: 2

NEXT

◁⟩ AT(3)_5

11

3:00

Type the missing letters to complete the text below.

Hydraulics are most commonly applied through a cylinder that contains an internal rod. The `r` [ ] is `c o n n` [ ] to a pusher `p l` [ ]. As `f l` [ ] flows `b e h` [ ] the `p u s` [ ] plate, the `r` [ ] is `p u s` [ ] outwards. The `b r a` [ ] in a car `p u` [ ] the `b r` [ ] pads `d o` [ ] when `f l` [ ] is `a p p` [ ]. Hydraulic cylinders also allow a backhoe to push and retract its bucket.

NEXT

12

1:00

Type the statement that you hear.

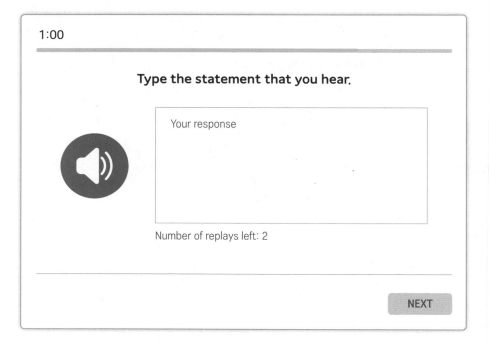

Your response

Number of replays left: 2

NEXT

◁)) AT(3)_6

13

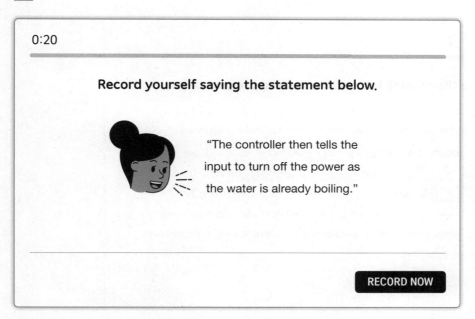

0:20

Record yourself saying the statement below.

"The controller then tells the input to turn off the power as the water is already boiling."

RECORD NOW

14

1:00

Type the statement that you hear.

Your response

Number of replays left: 2

NEXT

AT(3)_7

15

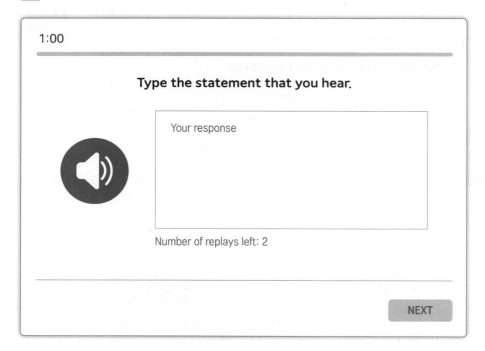

3:00

Type the missing letters to complete the text below.

Individuals are more likely to open and read a letter that is addressed specifically to them. Typing a group o[_] letters t h[__] are iden[____] except f[_] a f[__] minor cha[___] can b[_] very ti[__]-consuming. For th[_], we u[__] a fo[__] letter. Students should keep this in mind when sending out cover letters to universities and companies to which they are applying.

NEXT

16

◁)) AT(3)_8

1:00

Type the statement that you hear.

Your response

Number of replays left: 2

NEXT

17

0:20

Record yourself saying the statement below.

"This is when a memory can be hazy yet vivid, or haunting with perfect clarity."

RECORD NOW

18

1:00

Type the statement that you hear.

Your response

Number of replays left: 2

NEXT

Interactive Reading

This section will have 2 reading passages. For each passage, you will have 7 or 8 minutes to answer 6 questions.

NEXT

8:00   for the next 6 questions

PASSAGE

I designed a ① redesign / mascot / logo / shirt / sweatshirt for my friend's company now that she has ② started / made / found / gave / was to get more ③ businesses / customers / help / strategy / enough. I used some key concepts of logo design, ④ including / stating / being / of / showing brand identity, simplicity, and versatility. By using these ⑤ knowing / images / contrasts / concepts / signs, I felt that ⑥ how / new / to / another / my friend's logo could be unique and appealing to potential customers. I also wanted to make it look ⑦ up / out / professional / identical / create like other popular brand logos. I ⑧ followed / started / works / assist / came by designing a simple geometric figure based on a flower. I chose purple ⑨ on / by / the / as / over the main ⑩ flavor / focus / source / application / color to ⑪ deny / exact / emphasize / design / see wisdom and creativity.

Select the best sentence to fill in the blank in the passage.

① Select a word	∨
② Select a word	∨
③ Select a word	∨
④ Select a word	∨
⑤ Select a word	∨
⑤ Select a word	∨
⑥ Select a word	∨
⑦ Select a word	∨
⑧ Select a word	∨
⑨ Select a word	∨
⑩ Select a word	∨
⑪ Select a word	∨

NEXT

4:10   for the next 5 questions

PASSAGE

I designed a logo for my friend's company now that she has started to get more customers. I used some key concepts of logo design, including brand identity, simplicity, and versatility. By using these concepts, I felt that my friend's logo could be unique and appealing to potential customers. I also wanted to make it look professional like other popular brand logos. I started by designing a simple geometric figure based on a flower. I chose purple as the main color to emphasize wisdom and creativity.

Beneath the symbol, I wrote her company's name in an appealing typography that complemented the rest of the design.

Select the best sentence to fill in the blank in the passage.

- ○ It's also useful for designers who are creating logos for sports teams.

- ○ However, I need to create a variety of different designs for all my projects.

- ○ I only used three different shades of color to maintain the simplicity.

- ○ Looking back, I can see how I could have improved the logo design.

NEXT

3:40   for the next 4 questions

PASSAGE

I designed a logo for my friend's company now that she has started to get more customers. I used some key concepts of logo design, including brand identity, simplicity, and versatility. By using these concepts, I felt that my friend's logo could be unique and appealing to potential customers. I also wanted to make it look professional like other popular brand logos. I started by designing a simple geometric figure based on a flower. I chose purple as the main color to emphasize wisdom and creativity. I only used three different shades of color to maintain the simplicity. Beneath the symbol, I wrote her company's name in an appealing typography that complemented the rest of the design.

Click and drag text to highlight the answer to the question below.

Why did the author's friend need a logo for her company?

Highlight text in the passage to set an answer

NEXT

2:50   `for the next 3 questions`

PASSAGE

I designed a logo for my friend's company now that she has started to get more customers. I used some key concepts of logo design, including brand identity, simplicity, and versatility. By using these concepts, I felt that my friend's logo could be unique and appealing to potential customers. I also wanted to make it look professional like other popular brand logos. I started by designing a simple geometric figure based on a flower. I chose purple as the main color to emphasize wisdom and creativity. I only used three different shades of color to maintain the simplicity. Beneath the symbol, I wrote her company's name in an appealing typography that complemented the rest of the design.

Click and drag text to highlight the answer to the question below.

What two reasons did the author give for using logo design concepts in their work?

> Highlight text in the passage to set an answer

NEXT

2:00   for the next 2 questions

PASSAGE

I designed a logo for my friend's company now that she has started to get more customers. I used some key concepts of logo design, including brand identity, simplicity, and versatility. By using these concepts, I felt that my friend's logo could be unique and appealing to potential customers. I also wanted to make it look professional like other popular brand logos. I started by designing a simple geometric figure based on a flower. I chose purple as the main color to emphasize wisdom and creativity. I only used three different shades of color to maintain the simplicity. Beneath the symbol, I wrote her company's name in an appealing typography that complemented the rest of the design.

Select the idea that is expressed in the passage.

- ○ I think a logo should be simple yet easily recognizable by using unique colors and designs.

- ○ The main part of my friend's brand identity is the mascot, so I featured it in the logo.

- ○ I used concepts of logo design, such as simplicity and color, to create a logo for my friend's business.

- ○ The final step of designing an effective logo is choosing a color palette that conveys a specific feeling.

NEXT

1:00   for this question

PASSAGE

I designed a logo for my friend's company now that she has started to get more customers. I used some key concepts of logo design, including brand identity, simplicity, and versatility. By using these concepts, I felt that my friend's logo could be unique and appealing to potential customers. I also wanted to make it look professional like other popular brand logos. I started by designing a simple geometric figure based on a flower. I chose purple as the main color to emphasize wisdom and creativity. I only used three different shades of color to maintain the simplicity. Beneath the symbol, I wrote her company's name in an appealing typography that complemented the rest of the design.

Select the best title for the passage.

○ My Company's Logo

○ A Logo for My Friend

○ My Colorful Logo

NEXT

7:00   for the next 6 questions

PASSAGE

Who are the ideal people for a focus group? Researchers ① bring / came / gathered / have / help together a ② target / project / special / big / small group of six to twelve people to participate in a focus group and discuss specific commercial goods. Since focus groups ③ make / are / the / help / can quick to organize and easy for people to participate in, market research firms frequently ④ analyze / find / practice / use / teach them to learn about customer feelings ⑤ toward / from / to / buying / new a product.

Select the best sentence to fill in the blank in the passage.

① Select a word	∨
② Select a word	∨
③ Select a word	∨
④ Select a word	∨
⑤ Select a word	∨

NEXT

4:49   for the next 5 questions

PASSAGE

Who are the ideal people for a focus group? Researchers bring together a small group of six to twelve people to participate in a focus group and discuss specific commercial goods. Since focus groups are quick to organize and easy for people to participate in, market research firms frequently use them to learn about customer feelings toward a product.

As there are fewer people in a focus group, the small size encourages participants to be open with their opinions, whereas they may remain quiet in larger groups. With more willingness to communicate, focus group members are more likely to share their true feelings about the topic. The information obtained from focus groups has many applications in marketing. A focus group can help a company improve an existing product, explore potential product designs, or estimate the success of an upcoming product.

Select the best sentence to fill in the blank in the passage.

- Management and event planners may also utilize them to gather feedback that helps them to improve their services.

- The target demographic of a product and its placement in a store is called its position.

- Consumer behavior is influenced by both psychological and behavioral factors that motivate choice.

- Successful marketing is proactive marketing, so a company must expose new products to potential customers as soon as possible.

NEXT

PASSAGE

Who are the ideal people for a focus group? Researchers bring together a small group of six to twelve people to participate in a focus group and discuss specific commercial goods. Since focus groups are quick to organize and easy for people to participate in, market research firms frequently use them to learn about customer feelings toward a product. Management and event planners may also utilize them to gather feedback that helps them to improve their services. As there are fewer people in a focus group, the small size encourages participants to be open with their opinions, whereas they may remain quiet in larger groups. With more willingness to communicate, focus group members are more likely to share their true feelings about the topic. The information obtained from focus groups has many applications in marketing. A focus group can help a company improve an existing product, explore potential product designs, or estimate the success of an upcoming product.

Click and drag text to highlight the answer to the question below.

What are some of the advantages of focus groups?

Highlight text in the passage to set an answer

NEXT

2:20   for the next 3 questions

PASSAGE

Who are the ideal people for a focus group? Researchers bring together a small group of six to twelve people to participate in a focus group and discuss specific commercial goods. Since focus groups are quick to organize and easy for people to participate in, market research firms frequently use them to learn about customer feelings toward a product. Management and event planners may also utilize them to gather feedback that helps them to improve their services. As there are fewer people in a focus group, the small size encourages participants to be open with their opinions, whereas they may remain quiet in larger groups. With more willingness to communicate, focus group members are more likely to share their true feelings about the topic. The information obtained from focus groups has many applications in marketing. A focus group can help a company improve an existing product, explore potential product designs, or estimate the success of an upcoming product.

Click and drag text to highlight the answer to the question below.

How can information from focus groups be used in marketing?

Highlight text in the passage to set an answer

NEXT

1:30   for the next 2 questions

PASSAGE

Who are the ideal people for a focus group? Researchers bring together a small group of six to twelve people to participate in a focus group and discuss specific commercial goods. Since focus groups are quick and easy to organize, market research firms frequently use them to learn about customer feelings toward a product. Management and event planners may also utilize them to gather feedback that helps them to improve their services. As there are fewer people in a focus group, the small size encourages participants to be open with their opinions, whereas they may remain quiet in larger groups. With more willingness to communicate, focus group members are more likely to share their true feelings about the topic. The information obtained from focus groups has many applications in marketing. A focus group can help a company improve an existing product, explore potential product designs, or estimate the success of an upcoming product.

Select the idea that is expressed in the passage.

○ Market research helps a company reach its target market.

○ Focus groups reveal customer beliefs and opinions to market researchers.

○ Market research involves gathering information about consumers' needs and behaviors.

○ Consumers can use market research to learn more about a company's goods and services.

NEXT

0:50   for this question

PASSAGE

Who are the ideal people for a focus group? Researchers bring together a small group of six to twelve people to participate in a focus group and discuss specific commercial goods. Since focus groups are quick and easy to organize, market research firms frequently use them to learn about customer feelings toward a product. Management and event planners may also utilize them to gather feedback that helps them to improve their services. As there are fewer people in a focus group, the small size encourages participants to be open with their opinions, whereas they may remain quiet in larger groups. With more willingness to communicate, focus group members are more likely to share their true feelings about the topic. The information obtained from focus groups has many applications in marketing. A focus group can help a company improve an existing product, explore potential product designs, or estimate the success of an upcoming product.

Select the best title for the passage.

- ○ Marketing and Focus Groups
- ○ Market Research on Competitors
- ○ Revealing Consumer Psychology and Behavior
- ○ Planning a Successful Ad Campaign

NEXT

Interactive Listening

This section will have 2 conversations. For each conversation, you will have 4 minutes to select 5-7 conversation turns and 75 seconds to write a summary.

NEXT

1

4:00   for the next 5 questions

You will participate in a conversation about the scenario below.

You are a student in a math class. You have an important exam coming up at the end of the month, but you are finding it hard to study for it because your housemates are too noisy. You approach your professor to ask for advice.

START

1-1

3:30   for the next 5 questions

Question 1 of 5

Pick the best option to start the conversation.

○ Excuse me, Professor. I'm afraid I won't be able to attend class today.

○ Hi, Professor. Can you let me know what topics will be covered in the exam?

○ Excuse me, Professor. I'd like to submit my math assignment.

○ Hi, Professor. I've just arrived for the math study group.

○ Hi, Professor. I have a bit of an issue I'm hoping you can help with.

NEXT

3:00   for the next 4 questions

Hi, Professor. I have a bit of an issue I'm hoping you can help with.

Listen closely! You can only play the audio clips once.

AT(3)_10_1

Question 2 of 5

Select the best response.

- ○ Yes, that's why I'm here. I need to get your advice on some useful sources for my essay. All of the books on the recommended reading list are already checked out.

- ○ Thanks. The thing is, I can't study properly at home because it's too hard to concentrate. I share a house with some other students, and they make too much noise.

- ○ I really appreciate the offer! By attending the additional classes, I'll have no problem getting fully prepared for the upcoming math exam.

- ○ No, I don't feel very confident about the exam at the end of the month. I'm still struggling to understand some of the more complicated equations.

- ○ That would be great. It's so hard to study with so much noise in the classroom. I really hope you can get the other students to work more quietly.

NEXT

2:30 · for the next 3 questions

 Sure. I'm always here to assist my students.

Thanks. The thing is, I can't study properly at home because it's too hard to concentrate. I share a house with some other students, and they make too much noise.

🔊 AT(3)_10_2

Question 3 of 5
Select the best response.

○ That would be great. They may listen to you more than they listen to me.

○ Actually, I have. But it doesn't seem to have made any difference at all.

○ I had considered that, but I just wouldn't be able to afford it.

○ Well, it's still a little noisy, but the renovation work is scheduled to end soon.

○ I really tried to understand the lecture, but there were several points that left me confused.

NEXT

2:00   for the next 2 questions

 Well, that's a problem. Have you tried explaining this to them and asking them to be quieter?

Actually, I have. But it doesn't seem to have made any difference at all.

AT(3)_10_3

Question 4 of 5
Select the best response.

○ That's true, but it doesn't open until 9 A.M., and I prefer to study in the morning before classes.

○ Okay, that's a great idea. Let's meet outside at 8 and grab a bite to eat first.

○ Yes, I've noticed a huge improvement in my grades since I stopped studying at home.

○ I checked all of the shelves in the journal section, but I still wasn't able to find them.

○ That might work for some people, but I find it difficult to focus while listening to music.

NEXT

1:30　　　for this question

In that case, why don't you try studying in the university library? That's always a calm, quiet environment for reading and studying.

That's true, but it doesn't open until 9 A.M., and I prefer to study in the morning before classes.

🔊 AT(3)_10_4

Question 5 of 5

Select the best response.

○ That would be great! I'll send it to you by e-mail.

○ Awesome! That would suit me perfectly!

○ I really appreciate it. I'll let her know.

○ In that case, I better start studying this evening.

○ Great! It's the second classroom on the left.

NEXT

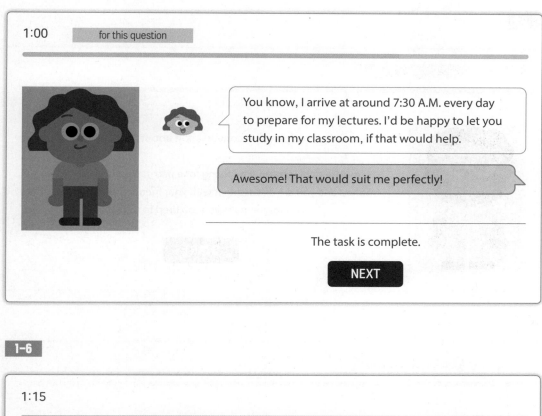

1:00   for this question

You know, I arrive at around 7:30 A.M. every day to prepare for my lectures. I'd be happy to let you study in my classroom, if that would help.

Awesome! That would suit me perfectly!

The task is complete.

NEXT

1-6

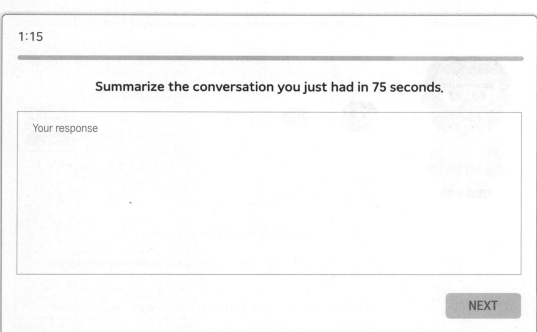

1:15

Summarize the conversation you just had in 75 seconds.

Your response

NEXT

4:00   for the next 5 questions

You will participate in a conversation about the scenario below.

You are thinking about applying for a part-time job to earn some money, and you are discussing it with your friend. You are worried that it might make you too tired to study.

START

3:30   for the next 5 questions

Listen closely! You can only play the audio clips once.

AT(3)_11_1

Question 1 of 5
Select the best response.

○ No, I don't think that would be a good idea for you.

○ It's funny you should say that because I've been looking for job vacancies.

○ Oh, that sounds interesting. How much are you paid per hour?

○ Actually, I don't have any regrets about accepting the job offer.

○ I think it's possible to attend evening classes instead of afternoon classes.

NEXT

3:00 for the next 4 questions

 Have you ever considered working part-time while you are here at university?

It's funny you should say that because I've been looking for job vacancies.

AT(3)_11_2

Question 2 of 5

Select the best response.

- ○ That's quite a lot of money. I'm not sure I'd be able to afford that.

- ○ You could apply for a student loan if you are struggling with your expenses.

- ○ Yes, and the job is located really close to my apartment, too.

- ○ Well, I appreciate the offer, but I'm not really interested in that type of work.

- ○ I did think about that, but I'm concerned that it could make me too tired to study.

NEXT

2:30   for the next 3 questions

 Oh, really? I was thinking about doing that, too. It would be a great way to earn some money.

I did think about that, but I'm concerned that it could make me too tired to study.

🔊 AT(3)_11_3

Question 3 of 5

Select the best response.

○ That would be perfect, but most of the jobs I've found are Monday to Friday evenings.

○ Thanks a lot for the invitation, but I'm afraid I already made plans for this weekend.

○ That sounds exhausting. I think I'll just stay at home and relax this evening.

○ Well, I suppose I could submit the application and see if I get invited for an interview.

○ I totally understand. I'll try to organize something for later in the week then.

NEXT

2:00   for the next 2 questions

 As long as it's just a part-time job, it shouldn't make you too tired. Maybe you could just work on weekends.

That would be perfect, but most of the jobs I've found are Monday to Friday evenings.

AT(3)_11_4

Question 4 of 5

Select the best response.

- ○ Thanks, that was a really useful web page. I found a lot of valuable information there.

- ○ I'm planning on doing that tonight. So far, I've just checked for jobs in the university newspaper.

- ○ Let's meet in the morning before class and we can grab a bite to eat first.

- ○ Try going to bed a little bit earlier every night. That really helps me to concentrate during classes.

- ○ Oh, that's a great idea. I've always wanted to get a job related to website design.

NEXT

1:30   for this question

 Hmm… that wouldn't be great. If you work late, you'll be tired for classes in the morning. Have you tried searching some websites for weekend work?

I'm planning on doing that tonight. So far, I've just checked for jobs in the university newspaper.

🔊 AT(3)_11_5

Question 5 of 5
Select the best response.

○ Thanks for your advice. I'll read over it tonight and return it to you tomorrow.

○ You're right. Perhaps it would be best to just get a job after I graduate.

○ I hear what you're saying, but I don't think they are open for business on weekends.

○ I definitely will. In fact, I'll share some links with you in case you're interested in them, too.

○ Well, I'll try to get their contact details for you so that you can submit your application form.

NEXT

1:00   for this question

Well, I still think it would be a great idea, assuming you can find a job on the weekends. Let me know what you find out after checking online.

I definitely will. In fact, I'll share some links with you in case you're interested in them, too.

The task is complete.

NEXT

2-6

1:15

Summarize the conversation you just had in 75 seconds.

Your response

NEXT

0:15

Writing

This section will have 4 writing questions: 3 Write About the Photo and 1 Interactive Writing. It will take up to 11 minutes.

NEXT

1

Write a description of the image below for 1 minute.

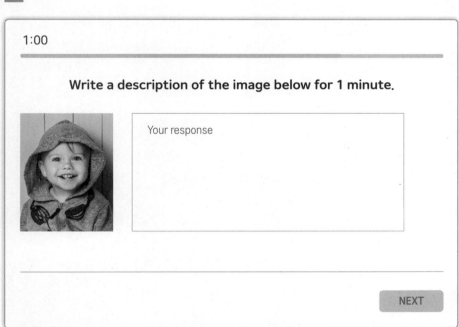

Your response

NEXT

2

1:00

Write a description of the image below for 1 minute.

Your response

NEXT

3

1:00

Write a description of the image below for 1 minute.

Your response

NEXT

4

5:00

❶ **Write about the topic below for 5 minutes.**   ❷ **Write a follow-up response for 3 minutes.**

People often take up hobbies to relax or
de-stress. Should employers help people
to pursue their hobbies to ensure a better
work-life balance? Give reasons for your
answer.

> Your response

CONTINUE AFTER 3 MINUTES

3:00

✔ **Write about the topic below for 5 minutes.**   ❷ **Write a follow-up response for 3 minutes.**

People often take up hobbies to relax or
de-stress. Should employers help people
to pursue their hobbies to ensure a better
work-life balance? Give reasons for your
answer.

> Your response

Do you believe that employers supporting
hobbies could enhance employee creativity?
Why or why not?

> Your response

CONTINUE AFTER 1 MINUTE

0:15

Speaking

This section will have 4 speaking questions. For each question, you will have 20 seconds to prepare and 90 seconds to respond.

NEXT

1

0:20

Prepare to speak about the topic below.
You will have 90 seconds to speak.

Number of replays left: 2

RECORD NOW

🔊 AT(3)_12

1:30

Speak about the topic for 90 seconds.

Number of replays left: 0

● RECORDING...   YOU CAN CONTINUE AFTER 30 SECONDS

2

0:20

Prepare to speak about the image below.

You will have 90 seconds to speak.

RECORD NOW

1:30

Speak about the image below for 90 seconds.

● RECORDING... ⅈⅉⅈⅉⅈ YOU CAN CONTINUE AFTER 30 SECONDS

3

0:20

Prepare to speak about the topic below.

You will have 90 seconds to speak.

> **Describe something you have done that you would not normally do.**
>
> • Why did you do it?
> • How did it affect you?
> • If you could go back in time, would you do it again?
> • Why or why not?

RECORD NOW

1:30

Speak about the topic below for 90 seconds.

> **Describe something you have done that you would not normally do.**
>
> • Why did you do it?
> • How did it affect you?
> • If you could go back in time, would you do it again?
> • Why or why not?

● RECORDING... YOU CAN CONTINUE AFTER 30 SECONDS

4

AT(3)_13

0:20

Prepare to speak about the topic below.
You will have 90 seconds to speak.

Number of replays left: 2

RECORD NOW

1:30

Speak about the topic for 90 seconds.

Number of replays left: 0

● RECORDING...　　　　YOU CAN CONTINUE AFTER 30 SECONDS

0:15

Writing & Speaking Sample

This section will have a writing question and a speaking question. These 2 questions will contribute to your score and will also be available to the institutions that receive your results.

NEXT

0:30

Prepare to write about the topic below.

You will have 5 minutes to write.

> Some people feel that college is a time to explore their interests and try new activities. Others think that their time is better spent practicing what they are already good at and gaining greater expertise. Which stance do you agree with more? Why? What are some pros and cons to this way of approaching college?

START

5:00

Write about the topic below for 5 minutes.

Some people feel that college is a time to explore their interests and try new activities. Others think that their time is better spent practicing what they are already good at and gaining greater expertise. Which stance do you agree with more? Why? What are some pros and cons to this way of approaching college?

Your response

YOU CAN CONTINUE AFTER 3 MINUTES

2

0:30

Prepare to speak about the topic below.

You will have 3 minutes to speak.

> Making decisions can be a difficult process. How do you make decisions? Do you weigh multiple factors before making a decision, or do you just go with your intuition? Why?

START

3:00

Speak about the topic below for 3 minutes.

> Making decisions can be a difficult process. How do you make decisions? Do you weigh multiple factors before making a decision, or do you just go with your intuition? Why?

● RECORDING... YOU CAN SUBMIT AFTER 1 MINUTE

Actual Test (3)
Answers

1	YES
2	NO
3	NO
4	NO
5	YES
6	NO
7	YES
8	NO
9	NO
10	NO
11	YES
12	YES
13	YES
14	NO
15	YES
16	NO
17	NO
18	YES

어휘

interest 관심, 흥미, 이자 circle 원 variety 다양성 differ 다르다 afraid 두려운 easily 쉽게 office 사무실 tropical 열대의

Fill in the Blanks

1 stop
비록 대화를 중단하고 싶었지만, 예의상 대화를 계속하고 있는 제 자신을 발견했습니다.

2 seating
학생들의 이름을 쉽게 외우기 위해, 그 교수는 좌석 배치도를 실시했습니다.

3 crying
케빈은 승진 소식을 들었을 때, 기쁨의 눈물을 흘릴 수밖에 없었습니다.

4 getaway
마을 외곽에 위치한 이 고풍스러운 커피숍은 그녀가 가장 좋아하는 주말 휴식처였습니다.

5 clip
결혼식에서 우리가 춤추는 영상을 제게 보내주실 수 있나요?

6 milestone
당신의 첫 승진은 중요한 이정표입니다.

7 batted
투수는 타자가 능숙하게 야구공을 쳐서 경기장을 가로지르는 모습을 지켜보았습니다.

8 sweaty
뙤약볕 아래서 오래 조깅을 하고 나니, 옷이 엄청나게 땀에 젖고 더러워졌습니다.

9 mile
여러분은 우리 구획이 거의 0.5평방 마일에 달한다는 사실을 알고 계셨습니까?

어휘

conversation 대화 out of politeness 예의상 memorize 외우다, 암기하다 institute 도입하다, 시행하다, 실시하다
seating chart 좌석 배치도 promotion 승진 cannot help -ing ~하지 않을 수밖에 없다 tears of joy 기쁨의 눈물
edge 외곽 quaint 고풍스러운, 예스러운 getaway spot 휴식처, 도피처, 안식처 video clip 비디오 영상 milestone
이정표 pitcher 투수 hitter 타자 skillfully 능숙하게 bat 방망이로 치다 across the field 경기장을 가로지르는 jog
조깅하다 incredibly 엄청나게, 믿을 수 없이 sweaty 땀에 젖은 subdivision 구획, 필지, 분양지 take up 차지하다
square 평방, 제곱 mile 마일(1mile≒1.6km)

SECTION Mixed Language Skills

1 I didn't know what was going to happen.
무슨 일이 일어날지 몰랐습니다.

2 송아지는 특히 머리와 등에 갈색 또는 붉은색 털이 있습니다.

3 My diaries cover 25 years.
제 일기에는 25년의 세월이 담겨 있습니다.

4 그는 그의 자금을 위한 수익성 있는 투자처를 찾았습니다.

5 Political philosophy as a discipline addresses the nature, scope, and legitimacy of legal authority and how people interact with it. It is sometimes thought of as a part of political science. It asks questions such as "What is the ultimate source of justice?" and "How does a government maintain its authority?"
학문으로서 정치철학은 법적 권한의 본질, 범위, 그리고 적법성과 사람들이 그것과 어떻게 상호작용하는지를 다룹니다. 그것은 때때로 정치학의 한 부분으로 여겨집니다. 그것은 "정의의 궁극적인 근본은 무엇인가?"와 "정부는 어떻게 권한을 유지 하는가?"와 같은 질문을 던집니다.

6 That's what's funny.
그것이 재밌는 것입니다.

7 결과적으로, 1990년대 중반 이후 주정부 수입이 14배 증가했습니다.

8 It will automatically jump to the store introduction page.
그것은 자동으로 그 매장 소개 페이지로 넘어갈 것입니다.

9 이 제품들은 휴대성을 위해 디자인된 1인용 포장의 조절된 양으로 종종 판매됩니다.

10 Sometimes, they had a refrain after each verse so that everybody could join in.
때로는, 모든 사람이 참여할 수 있도록 각 절 뒤에 후렴을 넣기도 했습니다.

11 Hydraulics are most commonly applied through a cylinder that contains an internal rod. The rod is connected to a pusher plate. As fluid flows behind the pusher plate, the rod is pushed outwards. The brakes in a car push the brake pads down when fluid is applied. Hydraulic cylinders also allow a backhoe to push and retract its bucket.
유압 장치는 내부 피스톤 봉이 들어 있는 실린더를 통해 가장 일반적으로 사용됩니다. 피스톤 봉은 추진기 판에 연결됩니다. 유체가 추진기 판 뒤로 흐를 때 봉은 바깥쪽으로 밀립니다. 자동차의 브레이크는 오일이 도포되면 브레이크 패드를 아래로 밀어냅니다. 또한 유압 실린더는 굴찾기가 버킷을 밀거나 접을 수 있도록 합니다.

12 The Salmonella bacteria are directly associated with the turtles.
살모넬라 박테리아는 거북이와 직접적으로 연관되어 있습니다.

13 이미 물이 끓고 있기에, 제어 장치는 그때 전원을 끄도록 입력 장치에 지시합니다.

14 These rewards are based on how well they meet those goals.
이 보상들은 이러한 목표를 얼마나 잘 달성하는지에 근거합니다.

15 Individuals are more likely to open and read a letter that is addressed specifically to them. Typing a group of letters that are identical except for a few minor changes can be very time-consuming. For this, we use a form letter. Students should keep this in mind when sending out cover letters to universities and companies to which they are applying.

사람들은 특별히 자기 앞으로 온 편지를 열어 읽을 가능성이 더 높습니다. 몇 가지 사소한 변경 사항을 제외하고 동일한 편지 뭉치를 타이핑하는 것은 시간이 많이 걸릴 수 있습니다. 이를 위해 우리는 편지 형식을 씁니다. 학생들은 그들이 지원하는 대학과 회사에 자기소개서를 보낼 때 이것을 명심해야 합니다.

16 The project was delayed because of a miscommunication within the management.
이 프로젝트는 경영진의 잘못된 의사소통으로 인해 지연되었습니다.

17 이것은 기억이 흐리지만 생생할 수 있거나, 완전히 선명하게 계속 떠오를 수 있는 때입니다.

18 She changed her schedule to match his.
그녀는 자신의 일정을 그의 일정에 맞춰 변경했습니다.

어휘

calf 송아지 brownish 갈색의 reddish 붉은색의 hair 털 back 등 diary 일기 cover 담다 look for 찾다 profitable 수익성 있는 investment 투자(처) capital 자금, 자본금 political philosophy 정치 철학 discipline 학문의 분야 nature 본질, 특징 scope 범위, 영역 legitimacy 적법성, 합법성 legal authority 법적 권한 interact with ~와 상호 작용을 하다 political science 정치학 ultimate 궁극적인 source 근원, 근본, 출처 authority 권한 as a result 결과적으로 state 국가, 나라, (미국 등에서의) 주 revenue 수익, 세입 automatically 자동으로 introduction 소개 portion 부분, 1인분 controlled 관리된, 조정된 single serve 1인용의 packaging 포장 portability 휴대성 refrain 후렴 verse (노래의) 절 hydraulic n. 수압[유압] 응용 기계 a. 수압의, 유압의 cylinder 원통, 실린더 internal 내부의 rod 막대, 피스톤봉 pusher 추진기 plate 판, 판금 fluid 유체 brake pad 브레이크 패드 backhoe 굴착기 retract 집어넣다 bucket 들통, 버킷, 물통 salmonella 살모넬라균 bacteria 세균 directly 직접적으로 associated with ~와 관련된 controller 관리자, 제어 장치 input 입력 장치 reward 보상 based on ~에 근거한 meet a goal 목표를 달성하다 individual 개인, 사람 address to ~의 앞으로 보내다 time-consuming 시간 소모가 큰 form letter 같은 내용의 편지 keep in mind ~을 염두하다, 기억하다 cover letter 자기소개서 apply 지원하다 miscommunication 잘못된 의사소통 management 경영진 hazy 흐릿한 vivid 생생한, 선명한 haunt 계속 떠오르다, 출몰하다 clarity 선명, 명확성 match 맞추다

Actual Test (3) Answers

Interactive Reading

친구가 고객을 늘리기 시작했기 때문에 저는 친구 회사의 로고를 디자인했습니다. 저는 브랜드 아이덴티티, 심플함, 다양성등 로고 디자인의 핵심 개념을 사용했습니다. 이러한 컨셉들을 사용함으로써, 저는 제 친구의 로고가 독특하고 잠재 고객들 에게 어필할 수 있다고 느꼈습니다. 또한 그것이 다른 인기 브랜드 로고처럼 전문적으로 보이고 싶었습니다. 저는 꽃을 바탕 으로 간단한 기하학적 도형을 디자인하는 것으로 시작했습니다. 저는 지혜와 창의성을 강조하기 위해 보라색을 주색으로 선택했습니다. 저는 심플함을 유지하기 위해 세 가지 색조만 사용했습니다. 그 심벌 아래에, 저는 디자인 나머지를 보완하는 매력적인 서체로 그녀의 회사 이름을 적었습니다.

1-1   ① logo ② started ③ customers ④ including ⑤ concepts ⑥ my ⑦ professional ⑧ started ⑨ as ⑩ color ⑪ emphasize

1-2   (1) 그것은 또한 스포츠 팀을 위한 로고를 만드는 디자이너들에게 유용합니다.
(2) 하지만, 저는 제 모든 프로젝트를 위해 다양한 디자인을 만들어야 합니다.
(3) 저는 심플함을 유지하기 위해 세 가지 색조만 사용했습니다.
(4) 돌이켜보면, 로고 디자인을 어떻게 개선할 수 있었는지 알 수 있습니다.

1-3   *글쓴이의 친구는 왜 그녀의 회사에 로고가 필요했습니까?*

(now that) she has started to get more customers

1-4   *글쓴이가 작품에 로고 디자인 컨셉을 사용한 두 가지 이유는 무엇입니까?*

By using these concepts, I felt that my friend's logo could be unique and appealing to potential customers. I also wanted to make it look professional like other popular brand logos.

1-5   (1) 제 생각에 로고는 심플하면서도 독특한 색상과 디자인을 사용하여 쉽게 알아볼 수 있어야 합니다.
(2) 제 친구의 브랜드 아이덴티티는 마스코트가 주요 부분이라 그것을 로고에 넣었습니다.
(3) 친구 사업의 로고를 위해 심플함과 색상과 같은 로고 디자인 컨셉을 사용했습니다.
(4) 효과적인 로고를 디자인하는 마지막 단계는 특정한 느낌을 전달하는 색상 팔레트를 선택하는 것입니다.

1-6   (1) 내 회사의 로고
(2) 친구를 위한 로고
(3) 내 다채로운 로고

어휘

key 핵심의 concept 콘셉트, 개념 simplicity 평이함 versatility 다양성 potential customer 잠재 고객 brand 상표, 브랜드 geometric 기하학의 figure 도형 wisdom 지혜 appealing 매력적인 typography 서체 complement 보완하다 shade of color 색상 recognizable 쉽게 알아볼 수 있는 mascot 마스코트 convey 전달하다, 전하다

포커스 그룹에 이상적인 사람은 누구입니까? 연구원들은 6명에서 12명으로 구성된 소규모 그룹을 모아 포커스 그룹에 참여 하고 특정 상업용 상품에 대해 논의합니다. 포커스 그룹은 빠르고 쉽게 구성할 수 있기 때문에, 시장 조사 회사들은 제품에 대한 고객의 감정에 대해 알기 위해 포커스 그룹을 자주 사용합니다. 관리자 및 이벤트 기획자는 서비스 개선에 도움이 되는 피드백을 수집하기 위해 이를 활용할 수도 있습니다. 포커스 그룹에 더 적은 수의 사람들이 있기 때문에, 작은 규모는 참가 자들이 자신의 의견에 대해 개방적이게 하는 반면, 더 큰 그룹에서는 참가자들이 조용히 있을 수 있습니다. 의사소통에 대한 의지가 더 높아지면 포커스 그룹 구성원들은 주제에 대한 그들의 진실한 감정을 공유할 가능성이 높습니다. 포커스 그룹으 로부터 얻은 정보는 마케팅에 많이 응용될 수 있습니다. 포커스 그룹은 기업이 기존 제품을 개선하거나, 잠재적인 제품 디자 인을 탐색하거나, 신제품의 성공을 예측하는데 도움이 될 수 있습니다.

2-1 ① bring ② small ③ are ④ use ⑤ toward

2-2 (1) 관리자 및 이벤트 기획자는 서비스 개선에 도움이 되는 피드백을 수집하기 위해 이를 활용할 수도 있습니다.

(2) 제품의 타겟 인구와 제품의 상점에서의 배치를 포지션이라고 합니다.

(3) 소비자 행동은 선택에 동기를 부여하는 심리적, 행동적 요인 모두에 의해 영향을 받습니다.

(4) 성공적인 마케팅은 프로액티브 마케팅이므로, 기업은 가능한 한 빨리 잠재 고객에게 신제품을 출시켜야 합니다.

2-3 포커스 그룹의 장점은 무엇입니까?

focus groups are quick to organize and easy for people to participate in

2-4 포커스 그룹의 정보를 마케팅에 어떻게 사용할 수 있습니까?

A focus group can help a company improve an existing product, explore potential product designs, or estimate the success of an upcoming product.

2-5 (1) 시장 조사는 기업이 목표 시장에 도달하는 데 도움이 됩니다.

(2) 포커스 그룹은 고객의 신념과 의견을 시장 조사원에게 공개합니다.

(3) 시장 조사는 소비자의 요구와 행동에 대한 정보를 수집하는 것을 포함합니다.

(4) 소비자들은 회사의 상품과 서비스에 대해 더 많이 알기 위해 시장 조사를 사용할 수 있습니다.

2-6 (1) 마케팅 및 포커스 그룹

(2) 경쟁업체에 대한 시장 조사

(3) 소비자의 심리와 행동을 드러내기

(4) 성공적인 광고 캠페인 계획

어휘

focus group 포커스 그룹(각 계층을 대표하도록 선출한 소수의 사람들로 이루어진 그룹) whereas ~에 반하여, 그러나 willingness 기꺼이 하는 마음 obtain 얻다 application 응용, 적용 estimate 추정하다 upcoming product 새로 나올 제품 demographic 인구의, 인구 통계의 placement 배치 consumer behavior 소비자 행동 proactive 상황을

앞서서 주도하는, 미리 대책을 강구하는 **market research** 시장 조사 **involve** 수반하다, 포함하다

SECTION   Interactive Listening

> **당신은 아래 주제에 대한 대화에 참여하게 됩니다.**
>
> 당신은 수학 수업을 듣는 학생입니다. 월말에 중요한 시험이 다가오는데 동거인들이 너무 시끄러워서 공부하기가 어렵습니다. 교수님께 조언을 구하기 위해 교수님께 다가갑니다.

1-1
(1) 실례합니다, 교수님. 오늘 수업에 참석할 수 없을 것 같습니다.
(2) 안녕하세요, 교수님. 시험에서 어떤 주제가 다뤄질지 알려주실 수 있을까요?
(3) 실례합니다, 교수님. 수학 과제를 제출하고 싶습니다.
(4) 안녕하세요, 교수님. 수학 스터디 그룹에 방금 도착했습니다.
(5) 안녕하세요, 교수님. 교수님께서 도와주셨으면 하는 문제가 있습니다.

(음원) 물론입니다. 저는 항상 학생들을 돕기 위해 여기에 있습니다.

1-2
(1) 네, 그래서 제가 여기 온 것입니다. 에세이에 유용한 소스에 대한 조언이 필요합니다. 추천 읽기 목록에 있는 모든 책은 이미 대출되어 있습니다.
(2) 감사합니다. 문제는, 집중하기가 너무 힘들어서 집에서는 제대로 공부할 수 없습니다. 다른 학생들과 집을 같이 사용하는데 너무 시끄럽습니다.
(3) 제안을 주셔서 정말 감사합니다! 추가 수업에 참석하면 다가오는 수학 시험에 완벽하게 대비하는 데 아무런 문제가 없을 것입니다.
(4) 아니요, 월말에 있을 시험에 대해 자신감이 없습니다. 저는 아직도 좀 더 복잡한 방정식을 이해하는 데 어려움을 겪고 있습니다.
(5) 그러면 정말 좋을 것 같습니다. 교실이 너무 시끄러워서 공부하기가 너무 힘듭니다. 다른 학생들이 좀 더 조용히 일할 수 있도록 도와주셨으면 좋겠습니다.

(음원) 네, 그게 문제이네요. 혹시 설명하고 조용이 해달라고 요청해 보셨나요?

1-3
(1) 그러면 정말 좋을 것 같습니다. 제 말보다 교수님 말을 더 들을 것 같습니다.
(2) 사실, 이미 했습니다. 하지만 전혀 차이가 없는 것 같습니다.
(3) 고려는 해봤지만, 감당할 수 있는 여력이 되지 않습니다.
(4) 네, 여전히 조금 시끄럽지만, 보수 공사가 곧 끝날 예정입니다.
(5) 강의를 정말 이해하려고 노력했지만, 하지만 몇 가지 혼란스러운 점들이 있었습니다.

(음원) 그런 경우에는, 대학 도서관에서 공부해보는 건 어떨까요? 항상 조용하고 차분한 환경에서 독서와 공부를 할 수 있습니다.

1-4　(1) 맞습니다, 하지만 오전 9시에 문을 열고, 저는 오전 수업 전에 공부하는 것을 선호합니다.
　　　(2) 네, 좋은 생각입니다. 8시에 밖에서 만나서 간단히 식사부터 하죠.
　　　(3) 네, 집에서 공부하는 것을 중단한 후 성적이 크게 향상되었습니다.
　　　(4) 저널 섹션의 모든 선반을 확인했지만 여전히 찾을 수 없었습니다.
　　　(5) 어떤 사람들에게는 효과가 있을 수 있지만, 저는 음악을 들을 때 집중하는 것을 어려워합니다.

(음원) 있잖아요, 저는 매일 아침 7시 30분경에 도착해 강의 준비를 합니다. 도움이 된다면, 제 강의실에서 공부할 수 있도록 해드리겠습니다.

1-5　(1) 그럼 정말 좋겠네요! 이메일로 보내드리겠습니다.
　　　(2) 아주 좋습니다! 저한테 딱 맞을 것 같아요!
　　　(3) 정말 감사합니다. 제가 그녀에게 알리겠습니다.
　　　(4) 그런 경우엔, 오늘 저녁부터 공부를 시작해야겠네요.
　　　(5) 잘됐네요! 왼쪽에 있는 두 번째 강의실입니다.

1-6　I was speaking to my professor because I was finding it too hard to study at home due to my noisy housemates. She suggested that I talk to my housemates about it, but I explained that I already had. She also suggested studying in the library, but it opens too late. In the end, she let me study in her classroom, which was a great solution.

나는 동거인들이 너무 시끄러워서 공부하기 어려워 교수님과 논의했습니다. 교수님은 내가 동거인들과 이야기를 나눈 것을 제안했지만, 이미 그렇게 했다고 말씀드렸습니다. 교수님은 도서관에서 공부할 것을 제안했지만 도서관은 너무 늦게 문을 엽니다. 결국, 강의실에 공부할 수 있게 해줬는데, 정말 좋은 해결책이었습니다.

모범답안 분석

도입부 내용 한 문장:	I was speaking to my professor because I was finding it too hard to study at home due to my noisy housemates.
대화 핵심 내용 두 문장:	She suggested that I talk to my housemates about it, but I explained that I already had. She also suggested studying in the library, but it opens too late.
결론/마무리 한 문장:	In the end, she let me study in her classroom, which was a great solution.

어휘

housemate 동거인 **submit** 제출하다 **check out** (도서관 책을) 대출하다 **properly** 제대로 **upcoming** 다가오는 **confident** 자신 있는 **complicated** 복잡한 **equation** 방정식 **renovation** 보수(작업) **grab a bite to eat** (간단히) 식사하다

> **당신은 아래 주제에 대한 대화에 참여하게 됩니다.**
>
> 당신은 돈을 벌기 위해 아르바이트를 구하는 것에 대해 친구와 논의하고 있습니다.
>
> 당신은 아르바이트로 인해 공부하기에 너무 피곤하지 않을까 걱정하고 있습니다.

(음원) 대학 재학 중 아르바이트 하는 것을 고려해 본 적이 있어?

2-1
    (1) 아니, 너에게 좋은 생각이 아닌 것 같아.
    (2) 마침 네가 말해서 하는 말인데 지금 일자리를 찾고 있었어.
    (3) 오, 흥미롭네. 시간당 급여는 얼마야?
    (4) 사실, 일자리 제안을 수락한 것에 대해 후회하지 않아.
    (5) 오후 수업 대신 저녁 수업에 참석할 수 있다고 생각해.

(음원) 아 정말? 나도 그렇게 할까 생각 중이었어. 돈을 벌 수 있는 좋은 방법이야.

2-2
    (1) 꽤 큰 금액이야. 내가 감당할 수 있을지 모르겠어.
    (2) 지출에 어려움을 겪고 있다면 학자금 대출을 신청할 수 있어.
    (3) 맞아, 그리고 일자리가 내 아파트와 가까운 곳에 있어.
    (4) 제안은 고맙지만, 나는 그런 종류의 일에 별로 관심이 없어.
    (5) 그 생각을 했지만, 공부하기에 너무 피곤하게 만들지 않을까 걱정돼.

(음원) 아르바이트라면 너무 피곤하지 않을 거야. 주말에만 일할 수도 있어.

2-3
    (1) 완벽할 것 같은데, 내가 찾은 대부분 일자리들은 월요일부터 금요일 저녁에 있어.
    (2) 초대해줘서 고마워, 근데 아쉽게도 이번 주말에 이미 계획이 있어.
    (3) 피곤하겠네. 오늘 저녁에는 그냥 집에서 쉴 생각이야.
    (4) 뭐, 지원서를 제출하고 면접에 초대받을 지 볼 수 있겠네.
    (5) 완전히 이해해. 그럼 다음 주 후반에 뭔가 계획해 볼게.

(음원) 음, 좋지 않을 것 같아. 늦게 일하면, 아침 수업 때 피곤할 거야. 주말 근무를 위해 웹사이트를 검색해 보았어?

2-4
    (1) 고마워, 정말 유용한 사이트였어. 정말 좋은 정보들을 많이 찾았어.
    (2) 오늘 밤에 그렇게 할 계획이야. 지금까지는, 대학 신문에 있는 공고만 확인했었어.
    (3) 수업 전에 아침에 만나서 먼저 간단한 식사를 하자.
    (4) 매일 밤 조금 더 일찍 잠자리에 들도록 노력해봐. 수업에 집중하는 데 큰 도움이 돼.
    (5) 오, 정말 좋은 생각이야. 나는 항상 웹사이트 디자인과 관련된 일을 하고 싶었어.

(음원) 뭐, 주말에 일자리를 구할 수 있다고 가정하면 여전히 좋은 생각이라고 생각해. 온라인으로 확인한 후 알게 된 것을 알려줘.

2-5
    (1) 조언을 주어서 고마워. 오늘 밤에 읽어보고 내일 다시 돌려줄게.
    (2) 네가 맞아. 그냥 졸업하고 취직하는 게 최선일 것 같아.

(3) 네 말을 알겠지만, 주말에는 영업을 하지 않는 것 같아.

(4) 꼭 그렇게 할게. 그럼, 너도 관심이 있을 수 있으니 링크를 공유할게.

(5) 지원서를 제출할 수 있도록 연락처를 알아보려고 노력할게.

2-6 I was speaking with my friend about how I was thinking about finding a part-time job to earn some money, but I was worried that it would make me too tired to study. He thought it was a great idea and suggested that I find weekend jobs. When I mentioned that I could not find any, he advised me to search online. In the end, I decided I would try this and let him know if I find anything suitable.

나는 돈을 벌기 위해 아르바이트를 구하고 있지만 공부하기에 너무 피곤하게 만들지 않을까 걱정하고 있는 것에 대해 친구와 이야기를 나누고 있었습니다. 친구는 좋은 생각이라고 생각했고 주말 근무 일자리를 알아보는 것을 제안했습니다. 내가 찾을 수 없다고 말하니 그는 온라인에서 찾아보라고 조원했습니다. 결국, 나는 시도해보고 적합한 것을 찾으면 알려주기로 했습니다.

모범답안 분석

도입부 내용 한 문장: I was speaking with my friend about how I was thinking about finding a part-time job to earn some money, but I was worried that it would make me too tired to study.

대화 핵심 내용 두 문장: He thought it was a great idea and suggested that I find weekend jobs. When I mentioned that I could not find any, he advised me to search online.

결론/마무리 한 문장: In the end, I decided I would try this and let him know if I find anything suitable.

어휘

student loan 학자금 대출 expense 지출 exhausting 피곤한 organize (계획을) 세우다 grab a bite to eat 간단하게 먹다 concentrate 집중하다 assume 가정하다 open for business 영업하다 suitable 적합한

SECTION Writing

1 This is a photograph of two people jogging with their pet dog. In detail, the man is wearing a dark gray jacket, and the woman is wearing a light gray jacket. The dog is running beside them on a leash held by the man.

이것은 애완견과 함께 조깅하는 두 사람의 사진입니다. 자세히 보면 남자는 짙은 회색 재킷을 입고 있고 여자는 밝은 회색 재킷을 입고 있습니다. 개는 남자가 잡은 목줄에 매여 그들 옆에서 달리고 있습니다.

2 This is a photograph of a young boy smiling. In detail, he is wearing a gray hoodie. He has blue eyes and blonde hair, and he seems very happy. It looks like there is a blue fence behind him.

이것은 웃고 있는 어린 소년의 사진입니다. 자세히 보면, 그는 회색 후드티를 입고 있습니다. 그는 파란 눈과 금발 머리를 가지고 있으며 매우 행복해 보입니다. 그 뒤에 파란색 울타리가 있는 것처럼 보입니다.

3 This is a photograph of several tall buildings. In detail, the building in the center is a brick building that features many arches. There are two trees with green leaves in front of the building.

이것은 여러 고층 건물들을 찍은 사진입니다. 자세히 보면 중앙에 있는 건물은 많은 아치들을 특징으로 하는 벽돌 건물입니다. 건물 앞에는 녹색 잎이 달린 나무 두 그루가 있습니다.

4 *① 사람들은 종종 휴식을 취하거나 스트레스를 해소하기 위해 취미를 갖습니다. 고용주는 일과 삶의 균형을 위해 직원들이 취미를 추구할 수 있도록 도와야 합니까? 당신의 답변에 대한 이유를 제시하세요.*

In my perspective, it is beneficial for employers to help people to pursue their hobbies. The main reason is that hobbies ensure a better work-life balance, which boosts productivity. When workers have a chance to relax and de-stress through their hobbies, they are more focused when they are on the job and accomplish more tasks.

Another reason is that offering support for hobbies can help retain employees. This is because people are more likely to keep working at a company that supports their personal interests. Therefore, employers should support their employees in pursuing their hobbies for better productivity and employee retention.

제 생각에는 고용주가 직원들이 취미를 추구할 수 있도록 돕는 것이 유익하다고 생각합니다. 가장 큰 이유는 취미가 일과 삶의 균형을 보장하여 생산성을 향상시키기 때문입니다. 근로자가 취미를 통해 휴식을 취하고 스트레스를 해소할 기회를 가지면 업무에 더욱 집중하여 더 많은 업무를 완수할 수 있습니다.

또 다른 이유는 취미 생활을 지원하면 직원을 유지하는 데 도움이 될 수 있다는 점입니다. 사람들은 자신의 개인적인 관심사를 지원하는 회사에서 계속 일할 가능성이 더 높기 때문입니다. 따라서 고용주는 생산성 향상과 직원 유지를 위해 직원들이 취미를 추구할 수 있도록 지원해야 합니다.

② 당신은 고용주가 취미를 지원하는 것이 직원의 창의성을 향상시킬 수 있다고 생각합니까? 왜 또는 왜 그렇지 않습니까?

I believe that employers supporting hobbies enhances employee creativity. This is because hobbies, such as writing, playing sports, and solving jigsaw puzzles, often involve creative thinking. As a result, hobbies would positively affect employees' performance at work.

저는 고용주가 취미를 지원하는 것이 직원의 창의성을 향상시킨다고 생각합니다. 글쓰기, 스포츠, 직소 퍼즐 맞추기 등의 취미는 창의적인 사고를 수반하는 경우가 많기 때문입니다. 결과적으로 취미는 직원의 업무

성과에 긍정적인 영향을 미칩니다.

어휘

on a leash (목)줄에 매여 hoodie 후드티 blond(e) 금발 fence 울타리 several 여러 brick 벽돌 feature ~을 특징으로 하다 arch 아치형 구조물, 아치형 장식 beneficial 유익한 pursue 추구하다 ensure 보장하다 work-life balance 워라밸, 일과 삶의 균형 boost 향상시키다 productivity 생산성 de-stress 스트레스를 해소하다 accomplish 완수하다 retain 유지하다, 간직하다 personal interest 개인적인 관심사 retention 유지, 간직 involve 수반하다 creative thinking 창의적 사고 positively 긍정적으로 affect 영향을 미치다 performance 성과

SECTION Speaking

1 *Many people are interested in ways to prolong their lives. Does this interest you as well? Why or why not?*
많은 사람들이 수명을 연장하는 방법에 관심을 갖고 있습니다. 당신도 이에 관심이 있습니까? 왜 또는 왜 안 그런가요?

It is true that many people want to prolong their lives. However, I am more interested in my quality of life than simply living longer. To me, I don't want to live a long life if it's accompanied by poor health or reduced cognitive function. That's why I try to look after my health by eating clean and exercising regularly to stay in shape. Additionally, I try to stimulate my mind by reading at least one book a month and playing board games with my family. To conclude, I am more interested in enjoying the benefits of good physical and mental health than prolonging my life.

많은 사람들이 수명을 연장하고 싶어하는 것은 사실입니다. 하지만 저는 단순히 오래 사는 것보다 삶의 질에 더 관심이 많습니다. 건강이 나빠지거나 인지 기능이 저하된다면 장수를 누리고 싶지 않습니다. 그래서 저는 건강한 식습관과 규칙적인 운동으로 건강을 관리하고 몸매를 유지하려고 노력합니다. 또한 한 달에 한 권 이상의 책을 읽고 가족과 함께 보드게임을 하며 정신적 자극을 받으려고 노력합니다. 결론적으로, 저는 수명을 늘리는 것보다 신체적, 정신적 건강의 혜택을 누리는 데 더 관심이 많습니다.

2 This is a picture of a little girl chasing pigeons. In detail, I can see that she is wearing a bright red coat. On top of that, she is smiling, and her arms are outstretched. From this, I can infer that she is having a lot of fun. And in the background, there are some store windows. This clearly shows that the girl is in a plaza.

이것은 비둘기를 쫓는 어린 소녀의 사진입니다. 자세히 보면, 소녀가 밝은 빨간색 코트를 입고 있는 것을 볼 수 있습니다. 또한 그녀는 웃고 있고 팔을 뻗고 있습니다. 이를 통해, 그녀가 매우 즐거워하고 있다는 것을 유추할 수 있습니다. 그리고 배경에는, 상점 창문이 있습니다. 이것은 소녀가 광장에 있다는 것을 분명히

보여줍니다.

3 *평소라면 하지 않았을 일을 한 적이 있다면 설명하십시오.*
· 왜 그것을 했습니까?
· 그 행동이 자신에게 어떤 영향을 미쳤습니까?
· 시간을 되돌릴 수 있다면 다시 그 일을 하겠습니까?
· 왜 하거나 왜 안하겠습니까?

Recently, I went on a blind date. I had never gone on one before, so I was very nervous. Also, I'm very shy and don't really go on many dates, so this wasn't normal for me. But when one of my friends from work set the blind date up, I agreed because I wanted to step out of my comfort zone and try something new. I was nervous, but I had a nice time. I don't think I'll see the other person again, but I'm glad I did it because it demonstrated that I can overcome my shyness. However, I don't think I would do it again if I could go back in time. I prefer being friends with someone before going on a date with them.

최근에, 저는 소개팅을 했습니다. 저는 한 번도 소개팅을 해본 적이 없어서 많이 긴장했었습니다. 게다가, 저는 낯을 많이 가리고 데이트를 많이 하지 않기에, 이런 일이 저에게는 흔한 일이 아니었습니다. 하지만 회사 친구 중 한 명이 소개팅을 주선했을 때, 안락함에서 벗어나 새로운 것을 시도해보고 싶었기 때문에 동의했습니다. 긴장되긴 했지만 즐거운 시간이었습니다. 상대방을 다시 만날 것 같지는 않지만 수줍음을 극복할 수 있다는 것을 보여줬기에 데이트를 해서 기뻤습니다. 하지만, 시간을 되돌릴 수 있다면 다시는 하지 않을 것 같습니다. 저는 누군가와 데이트를 하기 전에 먼저 친구가 되는 것을 선호합니다.

4 *In what ways can public gardens improve communities and the lives of people who live there?*
어떤 방식으로 공공 정원은 지역사회와 그곳에 사는 사람들의 삶을 개선할 수 있습니까?

Public gardens greatly improve communities and the lives of people who live near them in several ways. First of all, it is a widely known fact that green spaces can reduce stress and promote mental health. Therefore, they're especially important in cities where people don't have much access to nature. A public garden could be the only way that someone in the city can appreciate nature. Secondly, children can experience and learn about the variety of plant life that is on display at a public garden. In this way, public gardens can provide educational opportunities. Therefore, public gardens are beneficial for the surrounding communities.

공공 정원은 여러 가지 면에서 지역사회와 그 근처에 사는 사람들의 삶을 크게 향상시킵니다. 우선, 녹지 공간이 스트레스를 줄이고 정신 건강을 증진할 수 있다는 것은 널리 알려진 사실입니다. 그러므로, 공공 정원은 사람들이 자연을 접할 기회가 많지 않은 도시에서 특히 중요합니다. 공공 정원은 도시에 사는 사람들이 자연을 감상할 수 있는 유일한 방법이 될 수 있습니다. 둘째, 아이들은 공공 정원에 전시된 다양한 식물을 경험하고 배울 수 있습니다. 이러한 방식으로 공공 정원은 교육적 기회를 제공할 수 있습니다. 그러므로, 공공 정원은 주변 지역 사회에 유익합니다.

어휘

prolong 연장하다 quality of life 삶의 질 accompanied by ~이 동반되는 reduced 저하된, 감소된 cognitive 인지의 function 기능 look after 돌보다 eat clean 건강하게(깨끗한 음식을) 먹다 regularly 규칙적으로 stay in shape stimulate 몸매를 유지하다 physical 신체적 mental 정신적 chase 쫓다 pigeon 비둘기 bright 밝은 outstretch 뻗다 infer 유추하다 have a lot of fun 매우 즐거워하다 plaza 광장 blind date 소개팅 go on a date 데이트를 하다 shy 수줍은, 낯을 많이 가리는 normal 흔한, 보통의 set up 주선하다 comfort zone 안락함, 편안함 nervous 긴장된 demonstrate 보여주다 overcome 극복하다 shyness 수줍음 community 지역사회 reduce stress 스트레스를 줄이다 promote 증진하다 appreciate 감상하다 display 전시 educational 교육적 surrounding 주변

SECTION   Writing & Speaking Sample

1   몇몇 사람들은 대학이 그들의 관심사를 탐색하고 새로운 활동을 시도하는 시기라고 느낍니다. 다른 사람들은 그들의 시간이 이미 잘하는 것을 연습하고 더 나은 전문 지식을 얻는 데 소비하는 것이 더 낫다고 생각합니다. 당신은 어떤 입장에 더 동의 하십니까? 왜 그렇습니까? 대학을 다루는 이러한 방식에 대한 장단점은 무엇입니까?

Some people think that students should use college to focus only on the skills they will need in their future careers, while others believe college should be a time for experimenting and exploring new interests. I agree with the latter.

Students should take advantage of the diverse resources at university since they have the rest of their lives to gain experience in their chosen fields. Universities provide access to a vast array of academic and professional disciplines. Being able to take classes in any of these fields is a unique opportunity that students can only take advantage of for a short amount of time.

In addition, students will be exposed to all kinds of different people from a multitude of backgrounds. By opening themselves up to all of these different perspectives, students can become better prepared for both their careers and the rest of their lives.

There are some downsides, however. Students may become too distracted to become proficient in one field, so some focus is necessary. In addition, since university tuition is exceedingly expensive, it may not be a good idea for students to devote too much time to random classes just out of curiosity.

어떤 사람들은 학생들이 장래 진로에 필요한 기술에 집중하기 위해 대학을 이용해야 한다고 생각하는 반면, 다른 사람들은 대학이 학생들의 새로운 관심사를 실험하고 탐구하는 시간이 되어야 한다고 생각합니다. 저는 후자에 동의합니다.

학생들은 남은 일생동안 자신이 선택한 분야에서 경험을 쌓을 수 있기 때문에 대학의 다양한 자원을 활용해야 합니다. 대학은 학문 및 전문 분야에 대한 광범위한 접근을 제공합니다. 이런 다양한 분야에서 수업을 들을 수 있다는 것은 학생들이 짧은 시간 동안 누릴 수 있는 특별한 기회입니다.

또한 학생들은 다양한 배경을 갖고 있는 여러 종류의 사람들을 만나게 될 것입니다. 이러한 모든 다양한 관점에 자신을 개방 함으로써 학생들은 자신의 경력과 남은 인생을 위해 더 잘 대비할 수 있습니다.

하지만 몇 가지 단점이 있습니다. 학생들이 딴 데로 집중하여 한 분야에 능숙해질 수 없을 수도 있어서 어느 정도의 집중은 필요합니다. 게다가 대학 등록금이 지나치게 비싸기 때문에 학생들이 단지 호기심 때문에 관련이 없는 수업에 너무 많은 시간을 할애하는 것은 좋은 생각이 아닐 수 있습니다.

2 *결정을 내리는 것은 어려운 과정일 수 있습니다. 당신은 어떻게 결정을 내립니까? 당신은 결정을 내리기 전에 여러 가지 요인을 저울질하나요, 아니면 그저 당신의 직관에 따르나요? 왜 그렇습니까?*

It seems like no matter what, we'll need to make some difficult decisions in our lives. It's unavoidable. Maybe it's a decision about where to go to school, or whether to take a job offer or not, or whether to move to a new city. I've had to make some big decisions lately, and honestly, I always struggle with making them. I don't think I'm a great decision-maker.

If I have a process, then it involves a lot of overthinking. I tend to worry a lot, and I consider all the consequences of my decision. Sometimes this is overwhelming. It's impossible to know every outcome of a decision, right? Still, I try to take everything into account. I remind myself to think of the positive outcomes, too, instead of just focusing on the potential negatives. If I can focus on the benefits of a decision, then I feel more confident. Even though I tend to struggle with making big decisions, I do believe that I end up making the right one, most of the time. So, maybe all the overthinking is worth it.

I often wish I were better at making quick decisions with my intuition. I think I have good intuition, too, so maybe I could save myself a lot of worry. But, I still believe that making decisions too quickly can get you into bad situations. And if you end up in a situation you don't like, then you'll have to make more decisions to correct it. I guess, in this way, I'm glad that I spend so much time considering all my options when I make a big decision.

Everyone has their own process. This one seems to work for me, so far at least.

어쨌든 우리는 인생에서 몇몇 어려운 결정을 내려야 하는 것 같습니다. 그것은 불가피합니다. 그것은 학교를 어디로 갈 것인가, 일자리 제안을 수락할 것인가 아닌가, 혹은 새로운 도시로 이사할 것인가에 대한 결정일 수 있습니다. 저는 최근에 중대한 결정을 내려야 했는데, 솔직히 저는 결정을 내리는 데 항상 어려움을 겪습니다. 저는 제가 훌륭한 의사 결정자라고 생각 하지 않습니다.

제게 절차가 있다면 그것은 과도하게 많은 생각을 하는 것을 포함합니다. 저는 걱정을 많이 하는 편이고, 제 결정에 따른 모든 결과를 고려합니다. 때때로 그것은 큰 부담이 됩니다. 어떤 결정의 모든 결과를 아는 것은 불가능하지 않습니까? 그럼에도 불구하고 저는 모든 것을 고려하려고 노력합니다. 저는 잠재적인 부정적인 면에만 초점을 맞추지 않고 긍정적인 결과에 대해서도 생각하기 위해 제 자신을 일깨웁니다. 만약 제가 결정의 이득들에 집중할 수 있다면, 저는 더 확신을 느낍니다. 비록 제가 중요한 결정을 내리는데 어려움을 겪는 경향이 있지만, 저는 제가 결국 대부분 옳은 결정을 내리게 된다고 믿습니다. 따라서 오래 고민하는 것은 그만한 가치가 있을 지도 모릅니다.

저는 종종 제 직감으로 빠른 결정을 내리는 것에 더 잘하길 바랍니다. 저는 제 직감이 좋다고 생각해서 어쩌면 걱정을 덜 수 있을지도 모릅니다. 하지만 저는 여전히 너무 빨리 결정을 내리는 것은 안 좋은 상황에 처하게 할 수 있다고 믿습니다. 그리고 원치 않는 상황에 처하게 된다면, 그것을 바로잡기 위해 더 많은 결정을 내려야 할 수 있습니다. 그렇기 때문에 전 제가 중요한 결정을 내릴 때 모든 선택지를 고려하는데 많은 시간을 할애하는 것이 좋은 것 같습니다.

누구나 자신만의 절차가 있습니다. 최소한 지금까지는 이 방식이 저에게 효과가 있는 것 같습니다.

어휘

the latter 후자 (the former 전자) take advantage of ~을 이용하다 diverse 다양한 resource 자원 gain experience 경험을 얻다, 경력을 쌓다 field 분야 vast 방대한 array 집합체, 배열 academic 학문의 professional 전문적인 discipline 지식 분야 a multitude of 다수의 open up ~을 가능하게 하다, 마음을 터놓다 perspective 관점, 시각 downside 부정적인 면 proficient 능숙한 tuition 학비 exceedingly 극도로 random 무작위의 curiosity 호기심 weigh 저울질하다, 무게를 재다 factor 요인 intuition 직감 no matter what 어쨌든, 막론하고 unavoidable 불가피한 big decision 큰[중요한] 결정 struggle with ~로 고심하다 decision-maker 의사 결정자 process 절차, 과정 overthink 너무 많이[오래] 생각하다 consequence 결과 overwhelming 압도적인, 대응하기 힘든 outcome 결과 take into account ~을 고려하다 potential ~될 가능성이 있는, 잠재적인 negative 부정적 측면 confident 확신하는, 자신감 있는 tend to ~하는 경향이 있다 end up 처하게 되다 so far 이 시점까지, 지금까지 at least 적어도, 최소한

필수어휘

500

기출 어휘 암기 노트

□	001	tenant	세입자
□	002	association	협회
□	003	resident	주민
□	004	discuss	논의하다
□	005	issue	n. 사안, 문제 v. 발급하다
□	006	affect	영향을 주다
□	007	cleanliness	청결
□	008	repair	n. 수리 v. 수리하다
□	009	relate to	~와 관련되다
□	010	productive	생산적인
□	011	antique	골동품
□	012	eloquent	웅변의
□	013	exempt	면제되는
□	014	approachable	접근하기 쉬운
□	015	cautiously	조심스럽게
□	016	take a photograph	사진을 찍다
□	017	cement	시멘트
□	018	decline	줄어들다
□	019	purple	자주색
□	020	drain	n. 배수관 v. 물을 빼내다
□	021	instead	대신에
□	022	in detail	자세히, 구체적으로
□	023	blonde(=blond)	금발인
□	024	dressed up	옷을 멋지게 차려 입은
□	025	give a speech	연설하다

☐	026	suggest	암시하다, 시사하다
☐	027	stage	무대
☐	028	representative	n. 대표 adj. 대표하는
☐	029	organization	단체
☐	030	crowd	군중
☐	031	diverse	다양한
☐	032	focus on	~에 집중하다
☐	033	historical	역사적인
☐	034	architecture	건축물
☐	035	woods	숲
☐	036	bare	잎이 떨어진, 헐벗은
☐	037	fall	n. 가을 v. 떨어지다
☐	038	organism	생물
☐	039	instinct	본능
☐	040	flee	달아나다
☐	041	move	감동시키다, 움직이다
☐	042	explain	설명하다
☐	043	in depth	깊이, 상세히
☐	044	property	부동산
☐	045	primarily	주로
☐	046	drive	조종하다, 운전하다, 작동시키다
☐	047	supply and demand	수요와 공급
☐	048	eraser	지우개
☐	049	giraffe	기린
☐	050	acquire	얻다

☐	001	gather	모이다, 모으다
☐	002	endure	견디다
☐	003	storm	폭풍우
☐	004	food shortage	식량 부족
☐	005	outbreak	발생
☐	006	voyage	항해
☐	007	flipper	물갈퀴, 지느러미발
☐	008	tray	쟁반
☐	009	expert	전문가
☐	010	nominee	후보
☐	011	bitter	맛이 쓴
☐	012	angle	각도
☐	013	pharmacy	약국
☐	014	penguin	펭귄
☐	015	opportunity	기회
☐	016	arrange	준비하다
☐	017	start off	시작하다
☐	018	eventually	결국
☐	019	fall in love with	~와 사랑에 빠지다
☐	020	cuisine	요리
☐	021	vow	맹세하다
☐	022	scientific community	과학계
☐	023	gain a better understanding of	~을 한층 더 잘 이해하다
☐	024	disease	질병
☐	025	hypothesis	가설

☐	026	increasingly	점점 더
☐	027	unlikely	가망이 없는, 믿기 힘든
☐	028	committee	위원회
☐	029	be composed of	~로 구성되어 있다
☐	030	elect	선출하다
☐	031	technology firm	기술 회사
☐	032	bilingual	두 개 언어를 사용하는
☐	033	official language	공용어
☐	034	percentage	비율, 백분율
☐	035	native speaker	원어민
☐	036	decade	10년
☐	037	while	~인데 반하여, ~하는 동안에
☐	038	province	(행정 단위) 주
☐	039	respectively	각각
☐	040	in contrast	대조적으로
☐	041	account for	(부분·비율을) 차지하다
☐	042	population	인구
☐	043	rate	비율
☐	044	excess	과잉
☐	045	apparently	듣자[보아] 하니
☐	046	restriction	제한
☐	047	adolescent	청소년
☐	048	wary	경계하는
☐	049	entrance	입구
☐	050	allocate	할당하다

□	001	tentatively	잠정적으로
□	002	unfounded	근거 없는
□	003	liberal	자유주의의, 자유로운
□	004	disdain	업신여기다, 무시하다
□	005	rapidly	빨리
□	006	abandoned	버려진
□	007	extra time	연장전
□	008	potentially	가능성 있게
□	009	penalty shootout	승부차기
□	010	focus	n. 초점, 집중 v. 초점을 맞추다
□	011	patience	인내심
□	012	comply with	~을 준수하다
□	013	technical standard	기술 표준
□	014	store	n. 가게 v. 보관하다, 저장하다
□	015	handle	n. 취급 방법 v. 다루다
□	016	hazardous	위험한
□	017	material	물질
□	018	scarcity	부족
□	019	surface	표면
□	020	obvious	분명한
□	021	activism	행동주의
□	022	solution	해결책
□	023	convincingly	설득력 있게
□	024	control over	~에 대한 통제
□	025	promote	촉진하다, 홍보하다

☐	026	independence	독립(심)
☐	027	volcanic eruption	화산 폭발
☐	028	at least	적어도
☐	029	commercial airplane	민간 항공기
☐	030	inadvertently	무심코, 의도치 않게
☐	031	ash cloud	화산재 구름
☐	032	sustain	(피해를) 입다
☐	033	damage	손상
☐	034	replace	교체하다
☐	035	long-term	장기적인
☐	036	aircraft	항공기
☐	037	accumulation	축적
☐	038	sulfate	황산염
☐	039	deposit	침전물
☐	040	air force	공군
☐	041	fleet	함대, 비행대
☐	042	malign	비방하다
☐	043	alignment	가지런함, 정렬
☐	044	penniless	무일푼인
☐	045	principal	교장
☐	046	staff	직원
☐	047	improve	개선하다, 개선시키다
☐	048	gymnasium	체육관
☐	049	renovate	개조하다, 보수하다
☐	050	expand	확장하다, 확장시키다

☐	001	nationwide	전국적인
☐	002	dependent	의존하는
☐	003	graduate school	대학원
☐	004	shortage	부족
☐	005	enroll in	~에 등록하다
☐	006	renovation	보수, 수리, 혁신
☐	007	health clinic	개인 병원
☐	008	qualified	자격을 갖춘, 훌륭한
☐	009	physician's assistant	보조 의사, 대진 의사
☐	010	certified	면허증을 가진, 공인된
☐	011	critical	대단히 중요한, 위태로운
☐	012	examine	관찰하다
☐	013	patient	환자
☐	014	diagnose	진단하다
☐	015	illness	질환
☐	016	treatment plan	치료 계획
☐	017	minor	작은, 심각하지 않은
☐	018	injury	부상
☐	019	licensed	면허증/자격증을 소지한
☐	020	perform surgery	수술을 (집도)하다
☐	021	confidential	비밀의, 기밀의
☐	022	specialization	전문화
☐	023	expertise	전문 지식, 전문 기술
☐	024	routine duty	일상 업무
☐	025	workplace	직장

	026	prominent	중요한, 두드러진
☐	026	prominent	중요한, 두드러진
☐	027	advantage	장점, 이점
☐	028	allow A to B	A가 B하게 해주다
☐	029	social skills	사회적 능력
☐	030	broaden one's horizons	~의 시야를 넓히다
☐	031	interact	교류하다
☐	032	cooperate	협력하다
☐	033	communicate	소통하다
☐	034	extend	확장하다
☐	035	get a chance to	~할 기회를 가지다
☐	036	perspective	관점
☐	037	large family	다자녀 가정
☐	038	get along with	~와 잘 지내다
☐	039	characteristic	특성
☐	040	community	공동체
☐	041	come to mind	생각이 떠오르다
☐	042	lack	n. 부족 v. 부족하다
☐	043	privacy	사생활
☐	044	drawback	단점, 문제점
☐	045	opposite	반대의
☐	046	direction	방향
☐	047	foreground	전경
☐	048	sleeveless	민소매
☐	049	satisfied	만족한
☐	050	infer	짐작하다, 유추하다

☐	001	in need of	~가 필요한
☐	002	competent	능숙한, 잘하는
☐	003	thoroughly	완전히
☐	004	elaborate	더 자세히 설명하다
☐	005	reduce	줄이다
☐	006	misunderstand	오해하다
☐	007	positive reaction	긍정적인 반응
☐	008	encourage	장려하다
☐	009	commercial	n. 광고 adj. 상업의
☐	010	negative effect	부정적인 영향
☐	011	become aware of	알게 되다
☐	012	consequence	결과
☐	013	go on	~을 하다, 시작하다, 계속하다
☐	014	exposed	노출된
☐	015	pursue	추구하다
☐	016	inspire	고무하다, 영감을 주다
☐	017	admire	존경하다
☐	018	founder	창업자
☐	019	accomplishment	업적
☐	020	devote	(몸, 돈, 노력, 시간 등을) 바치다, 쏟다
☐	021	furthermore	더욱이
☐	022	influential	영향력 있는
☐	023	figure	숫자, 인물
☐	024	driving factor	원동력
☐	025	passionate	열정적인

☐	026	strive	정진하다, 매진하다
☐	027	follow in the footsteps of	~의 뒤를 따르다
☐	028	care about[for]	~에 마음을 쓰다
☐	029	tend to	~하는 경향이 있다
☐	030	depressed	우울한
☐	031	delighted	아주 기뻐하는, 아주 즐거워하는
☐	032	text	n. 글 v. 문자를 보내다
☐	033	screen	n. 화면 v. 가리다
☐	034	footbridge	보행자 전용 다리
☐	035	suspension bridge	현수교
☐	036	link	연결하다
☐	037	position	위치
☐	038	downstream	(강의) 하류
☐	039	upstream	(강의) 상류
☐	040	guideline	지침
☐	041	supervision	감독
☐	042	rewarding	보람 있는
☐	043	personnel	직원들, 인사과
☐	044	grasp	움켜잡다, 이해하다
☐	045	march	행진하다
☐	046	flag	깃발
☐	047	banner	현수막
☐	048	indicate	나타내다, 보여주다
☐	049	international	국제적인
☐	050	celebrate	기념하다

☐	001	multicultural	다문화의
☐	002	microphone	마이크
☐	003	dressed	옷을 입은
☐	004	casually	캐주얼하게, 격식을 차리지 않는
☐	005	long-sleeved	긴 소매의
☐	006	jeans	청바지
☐	007	frown	찡그리다
☐	008	melt	녹다
☐	009	keep -ing	계속 ~하다
☐	010	grievous	비통한
☐	011	disproportionate	불균형의
☐	012	welfare	복지
☐	013	assuredly	분명히
☐	014	specify	명시하다
☐	015	capacity	용량
☐	016	response	응답
☐	017	evolution	진화
☐	018	confusion	혼란
☐	019	depressing	우울하게 하는
☐	020	nuisance	골칫거리
☐	021	precisely	정확히
☐	022	plot	음모, 줄거리, 작은 구획의 땅
☐	023	mud	진흙
☐	024	due to	~에 기인하는, ~때문에
☐	025	nausea	메스꺼움

☐	026	settler	정착민
☐	027	take advantage of	~을 이용하다
☐	028	abundance	풍부
☐	029	coastal waters	연안 해역
☐	030	comet	혜성
☐	031	astronomer	천문학자
☐	032	observatory	관측소
☐	033	be located	위치하다
☐	034	approximately	대략
☐	035	faint	희미한
☐	036	object	물체
☐	037	magnitude	(별의) 광도, 중요도, 규모
☐	038	dim	어두운
☐	039	visible	보이는
☐	040	unaided eye	육안
☐	041	clearly	밝게, 또렷하게
☐	042	offspring	자식, 새끼
☐	043	perhaps	아마
☐	044	coherent	일관성 있는
☐	045	underneath	~의 밑에
☐	046	dissolve	녹다, 용해되다
☐	047	acidic solution	산성 용액
☐	048	include	포함하다
☐	049	meal special	특별 세트 메뉴
☐	050	for free	무료로

□	001	unfortunately	유감스럽게도
□	002	indifferent	무관심한
□	003	monetary	통화의
□	004	harshly	엄하게
□	005	fraudulent	사기를 치는
□	006	parallel	평행한
□	007	publish	출판하다
□	008	front cover	앞표지
□	009	depict	그리다, 묘사하다
□	010	spray	뿌리다
□	011	fuel passage	연료 통로
□	012	let	~하게 하다
□	013	sit	그대로 (방치되어) 있다
□	014	compressed air	압축 공기
□	015	blow out	불어내다
□	016	figure out	파악하다
□	017	circuit	회로
□	018	a face full of	~로 뒤덮인 얼굴
□	019	at this point	이 시점에서
□	020	repeat	반복하다
□	021	procedure	절차
□	022	electrician	전기 기사
□	023	fix	고치다
□	024	cable	전선
□	025	precedent	이전의

☐	026	workshop	작업장, 연수회
☐	027	cheery	쾌활한
☐	028	unreasonably	불합리하게
☐	029	considerate	사려 깊은
☐	030	amend	개정하다
☐	031	morale	사기, 의욕, 도덕
☐	032	crackdown	엄중 단속
☐	033	rhyme	운(음조가 비슷한 글자)
☐	034	disruptive	지장을 주는
☐	035	allocation	할당량
☐	036	silverware	은제품
☐	037	wholly	완전히
☐	038	persistence	고집, 끈기
☐	039	dispose	배치하다, 처리하다
☐	040	costly	많은 돈이 드는
☐	041	hydrogen	수소
☐	042	reputation	평판, 명성
☐	043	process	과정
☐	044	beer	맥주
☐	045	brewing	양조
☐	046	filter	거르다
☐	047	organic matter	유기물
☐	048	seawater	바닷물
☐	049	get into trouble	문제를 일으키다, 곤란에 처하다
☐	050	habit	습관

☐	001	safety	안전
☐	002	cool down	식히다
☐	003	air conditioner	에어컨
☐	004	urban	도시의
☐	005	section	부분
☐	006	open space	열린 공간, 공터
☐	007	set aside	따로 놓아두다
☐	008	recreational	레크리에이션의, 오락의
☐	009	natural ecosystem	자연 생태계
☐	010	maintain	유지하다
☐	011	city government	시 정부
☐	012	provide A for B	B에게 A를 제공하다
☐	013	green space	녹지 공간
☐	014	limit	n. 제한 v. 제한하다
☐	015	insect pest	해충
☐	016	feature	n. 특징 v. 특징으로 하다
☐	017	gardening	정원 가꾸기
☐	018	hiking trail	하이킹 코스
☐	019	sports facility	스포츠 시설
☐	020	public restroom	공중 화장실
☐	021	pond	연못
☐	022	social benefit	사회적 이익
☐	023	botanical garden	식물원
☐	024	native	토종의
☐	025	species	종

☐	026	give up	포기하다
☐	027	reality	현실
☐	028	ideology	이념
☐	029	statement	진술, 말
☐	030	bring about the best in	~의 최고의 모습을 끌어내다
☐	031	put efforts into	~에 노력을 기울이다
☐	032	outcome	결과
☐	033	satisfactory	만족스러운
☐	034	passion	열정
☐	035	bride	신부
☐	036	cancer	암
☐	037	involve	참여시키다, 참여하다, 수반하다
☐	038	non-profit organization	비영리 단체
☐	039	campaign	캠페인
☐	040	environmental issue	환경 문제
☐	041	aspect	측면
☐	042	groceries	식료품류
☐	043	irritate	짜증나게 하다
☐	044	react	대응하다, 반응하다
☐	045	interrupt	가로막다
☐	046	cut off	끊다
☐	047	repetitive	되풀이하는
☐	048	politely	정중하게
☐	049	conserve	보호하다
☐	050	commute	통근하다

☐	001	provide	제공하다
☐	002	air pollution	대기 오염
☐	003	place	n. 장소 v. 배치하다
☐	004	trash can	쓰레기통
☐	005	throw away	버리다
☐	006	install	설치하다
☐	007	environment	환경
☐	008	preserve	지키다, 보호하다
☐	009	minimize	최소화하다
☐	010	effective	효과적인
☐	011	plastic waste	플라스틱 폐기물
☐	012	biodegradable	생분해성의, 자연분해성의
☐	013	water bottle	물병
☐	014	ruin	망치다, 폐허로 만들다
☐	015	plant trees	나무를 심다
☐	016	shelter	은신처, 주거지
☐	017	bring about	~을 유발하다
☐	018	when it comes to	~에 있어서는, ~에 관해서라면
☐	019	bring together	모으다, 합치다
☐	020	crucial	중대한, 결정적인
☐	021	curriculum	교육과정
☐	022	subject	과목, 주제
☐	023	conclude	결론을 내리다, 끝내다
☐	024	interest	n. 관심, 이자 v. 관심을 갖게 하다
☐	025	variety	여러 가지, 다양성

	026	differ	다르다, 동의하지 않다
☐	027	political philosophy	정치 철학
☐	028	discipline	학문의 분야
☐	029	scope	범위, 영역
☐	030	legitimacy	적법성, 합법성
☐	031	legal authority	법적 권한
☐	032	interact with	~와 상호 작용을 하다
☐	033	ultimate	궁극적인
☐	034	source	근원, 근본, 출처
☐	035	mat	매트, 깔개
☐	036	blanket	담요
☐	037	hoodie	후드티(모자 달린 티셔츠, 점퍼)
☐	038	fence	울타리
☐	039	calf	송아지
☐	040	diary	일기, 메모장
☐	041	fragile	손상되기 쉬운
☐	042	protagonist	주인공
☐	043	hierarchy	계급, 지배층
☐	044	vivacious	명랑한, 쾌활한
☐	045	diarrhea	설사
☐	046	hydraulic	수압의, 유압의
☐	047	cylinder	원통, 실린더
☐	048	liberty	자유
☐	049	attic	다락(방)
☐	050	portion	부분, (1)인분

☐	001	portability	휴대성
☐	002	remorse	후회, 회환
☐	003	custody	양육권
☐	004	materialistic	물질 만능주의의
☐	005	concede	인정하다, 수긍하다
☐	006	rivalry	경쟁(의식)
☐	007	bribery	뇌물 수수
☐	008	recognition	인식
☐	009	stagger	휘청거리다, 깜짝 놀라게 하다
☐	010	tranquil	고요한, 평온한
☐	011	shabby	허름한
☐	012	appliance	장치, 기구
☐	013	speechless	(놀라거나 화나서) 말을 못 하는
☐	014	reassure	안심시키다
☐	015	subtle	미묘한
☐	016	refrain	n. 후렴 v. 삼가다
☐	017	verse	(노래의) 절
☐	018	fraud	가짜, 사기
☐	019	vomit	토하다
☐	020	illiterate	문맹의
☐	021	fertile	비옥한
☐	022	strenuous	힘이 많이 드는
☐	023	longing	갈망하는
☐	024	crude	n. 원유 a. 대충의, 미가공의
☐	025	legislation	제정법, 입법 행위

☐	026	dignity	위엄, 존엄성
☐	027	shrug	(어깨를) 으쓱하다
☐	028	hazy	흐릿한
☐	029	vivid	생생한, 선명한
☐	030	haunt	계속 떠오르다, 출몰하다
☐	031	per se	그 자체로는
☐	032	whereabouts	소재, 행방
☐	033	humiliating	굴욕적인
☐	034	conceited	자만하는
☐	035	dazed	(충격으로) 멍한, 아찔한
☐	036	underdeveloped	저개발의, 후진국의
☐	037	versatility	다양성, 다재다능
☐	038	geometric	기하학의
☐	039	typography	서체
☐	040	appealing	매력적인
☐	041	complement	보완하다
☐	042	demographic	인구의, 인구 통계의
☐	043	proactive	상황을 앞서서 주도하는, 미리 대책을 강구하는
☐	044	likes and dislikes	호불호
☐	045	appreciate	감상하다, 감사하다
☐	046	tuition	학비
☐	047	exceedingly	극도로
☐	048	intuition	직감
☐	049	weigh	저울질하다, 무게를 재다
☐	050	take into account	~을 고려하다